LSAT®

Writing Workbook

Other Kaplan Books for Law School Admissions

Kaplan LSAT: Premier Program

Kaplan LSAT: Comprehensive Program

Kaplan LSAT Logic Games Workbook

Kaplan LSAT Advanced

Kaplan LSAT Writing Workbook

Get Into Law School: A Strategic Approach

Law School Labyrinth: A Guide to Making the Most of Your Legal Education

LSAT®
Writing Workbook

The Staff of Kaplan Test Prep and Admissions

PUBLISHING

New York

LSAT® is a trademark of the Law School Admission Council, which neither sponsors nor endorses this product.

This publication is designed to provide accurate and authoritative information in regard to the subject matter covered. It is sold with the understanding that the publisher is not engaged in rendering legal, accounting, or other professional service. If legal advice or other expert assistance is required, the services of a competent professional should be sought.

© 2008 Kaplan, Inc.

Published by Kaplan Publishing, a division of Kaplan, Inc.
1 Liberty Plaza, 24th Floor
New York, NY 10006

Printed in the United States of America

October 2008
10 9 8 7 6 5 4 3 2 1

ISBN-13: 978-1-4277-9842-8

Kaplan Publishing books are available at special quantity discounts to use for sales promotions, employee premiums, or educational purposes. Please email our Special Sales Department to order or for more information at kaplanpublishing@kaplan.com, or write to Kaplan Publishing, 1 Liberty Plaza, 24th Floor, New York, NY 10006.

Table of Contents

KAPLAN

kaptest.com/publishing

The material in this book is up-to-date at the time of publication. However, the Law School Admissions Council may have instituted changes in the tests or test registration process after this book was published. Be sure to carefully read the materials you receive when you register for the test.

If there are any important late-breaking developments—or corrections to the content in this book—we will post that information online at kaptest.com/publishing. Check to see if there is any information posted there regarding this book.

kaplansurveys.com/books

What did you think of this book? We'd love to hear your comments and suggestions. We invite you to fill out our online survey form at kaplansurveys.com/books.

Your feedback is extremely helpful as we continue to develop high-quality resources to meet your needs.

The LSAT Writing Sample

Chapter 1: **About the LSAT Writing Sample**

The Writing Sample comes at the end of your LSAT day. Yes, you will be tired. Yes, you may feel like your brain is fried from the exam. But, with a little preparation you can rest assured that you will be able to whip up a first-rate Writing Sample with ease.

This chapter will give you a detailed overview of the Writing Sample, so you'll know a little more about what to expect. In Chapter 2, we'll review grammar, mechanics, and style, and Chapter 3 will show you how to write strong essays on test day. Chapter 4 will provide you with actual Writing Samples. In Chapter 5 we'll move from the Writing Sample to the personal statement required for law school applications.

WHAT IS THE LSAT WRITING SAMPLE?

So, what is the Writing Sample anyway? The Writing Sample consists of a scenario, or decision prompt, followed by two possible courses of action. You'll have 35 minutes to make a written case for your position. This section tests your ability to write a clean, concise, and persuasive argument. No outside knowledge whatsoever is required.

You will need to have a pencil to write the essay, as well as scratch paper, which will be provided by the exam proctor, to plan out your response before you actually write it. Your essay must be confined to the space provided on the Writing Sample Response Sheet, which is roughly the equivalent of two sheets of standard lined paper. You won't be given additional paper, so you'll have to keep your argument concise. Usually two or three paragraphs will be enough. Note that there's really no time or space to change your mind or radically alter your essay once you've begun writing, so *plan your argument out carefully before beginning to write.* Make sure to write as legibly as you can.

The Writing Sample is not graded, but it is sent to law schools along with your LSAT score. Many law schools use the Writing Sample to help make decisions on borderline cases or to decide between applicants with otherwise comparable credentials. Granted, it may not carry the same weight as the scored sections of the test, but since it can impact on your admission chances, your best bet is to take it seriously.

WHAT'S THE POINT?

You may wonder what the point of the Writing Sample is if it isn't graded. Well, once you enter law school, you will write essay after essay, and you will be required to analyze and summarize argument after argument. One of the main points of the LSAT Writing Sample is to assure law school admissions counselors that you will be able to handle the writing requirements by showing them that you can develop a concise, coherent argument even while under pressure (and taking the LSAT certainly does count as a pressure situation!).

SAMPLE ESSAY TOPIC

The following is an example of a Writing Sample topic:

The *Daily Tribune,* a metropolitan newspaper, is considering two candidates for promotion to business editor. Write an argument for one candidate over the other with the following considerations in mind:

- The editor must train new writers and assign stories.

- The editor must be able to edit and rewrite stories under daily deadline pressure.

Laura received a B.A. in English from a large university. She was managing editor of her college newspaper and served as a summer intern at her hometown daily paper. Laura started working at the *Tribune* right out of college and spent three years at the city desk covering the city economy. Eight years ago, the paper formed its business section, and Laura became part of the new department. After several years covering state business, Laura began writing on the national economy. Three years ago, Laura was named senior business and finance editor on the national business staff; she is also responsible for supervising seven writers.

Palmer attended an elite private college where he earned both a B.S. in business administration and an M.A. in journalism. After receiving his journalism degree, Palmer worked for three years on a monthly business magazine. He won a prestigious national award for a series of articles on the impact of monetary policy on multinational corporations. Palmer came to the *Tribune* three years ago to fill the newly created position of international business writer. He was the only member of the international staff for two years and wrote on almost a daily basis. He now supervises a staff of four writers. Last year Palmer developed a bimonthly business supplement for the *Tribune* that has proved highly popular and has helped increase the paper's circulation.

> ## RECENT LSAT WRITING SAMPLE TOPICS
>
> - Choosing between two candidates for a job, inheritance, or loan request
> - Choosing a method of expanding a business
> - Choosing between two plans or proposals

THE EIGHT BASIC WRITING SAMPLE PRINCIPLES

Here are the most important rules of thumb to remember when attacking the Writing Sample:

Principle 1: Use Scratch Paper to Plan Your Essay

The proctors give you scratch paper for a reason—so use it. Make yourself a rudimentary outline, listing the points you want to make in each paragraph. Ideally, you should know what you want to say and how you want to say it before putting pencil to paper.

Principle 2: Don't Obsess Over Your Position

Nobody really cares whether you consider the argument strong or which choice you make (for example, whether you choose to support Laura or Palmer in the sample essay topic on page 4). What's important is how well you support your position. Generally the decision alternatives are written to be pretty evenly matched, so there's no right or wrong answer, just a well-supported or ill-supported position.

Principle 3: Get Right to the Point

The first sentence should immediately offer a statement of your position. Assume that the reader is already familiar with the situation; there's no need to waste time describing the scenario.

Principle 4: Use a Clear, Simple Essay Format

Since you already know the structure of your essay topic, you can decide in advance how you will structure your response. One possibility is the "winner/loser" format, in which the first paragraph begins with a statement of choice and then discusses the reason why your choice (the winner) is superior. The next paragraph focuses on why the other alternative (the loser) is not as good and should end with a concluding sentence reaffirming your decision. Another possibility is the "according to the criteria" format, in which the first paragraph would discuss both the winner and the loser in light of the first criterion, and the second paragraph would discuss them both in light of the second criterion.

Whether you adopt one of these formats or use one of your own, the most important thing is that your essay be coherent in its reasoning. The more organized your essay is, the more persuasive it will be.

Principle 5: Mention, but Downplay, the Opposing View

Use sentence structures that allow you to do this, such as, "Even though Palmer won a prestigious national award . . ." and then attempt to demonstrate why this is really no big deal. This is an example of mentioning yet downplaying one of the loser's strengths. Try to do the same thing for at least one of the winner's obvious weaknesses. Doing so demonstrates that you see the full picture. Recognizing and dealing with possible objections will make your argument stronger.

Principle 6: Don't Simply Repeat Facts from the Prompt

Try instead to offer an *interpretation of the facts in light of the stated criteria.* If you're arguing for Laura in the Decision topic, you can't state simply that "Laura was named senior business and finance editor on the national business staff" and expect the reader to infer that that's a good thing. For all we know, being in that position may be a detriment when it comes to the criteria—training new writers and working under daily deadline pressure. It's up to you to indicate why certain facts about the winner are positive factors in light of the criteria, and vice versa for facts about the loser. Merely parroting what's written in the topic won't win you any points with the law schools.

Principle 7: Write Well

It sounds obvious, of course, but you should try to make your prose as clean and flawless as you can. Some people get so entangled in content that they neglect the mechanics of essay writing. But spelling, grammar, and writing mechanics are important. Use structural signals to keep your writing fluid and clear, and use transitions between paragraphs to keep the entire essay unified. Chapter 2: Essential Writing Skills provides an in-depth review of basic grammar, mechanics, and style. Sharpen your skills by spending some time reading through that chapter and answering the practice questions.

Above all, write or print legibly. In order to ensure that you have enough space for your essay on the Writing Sample Response Sheet, keep your handwriting to a reasonable size and write on every line provided.

Principle 8: Budget Your Time Wisely

We suggest spending roughly five to seven minutes reading the topic and planning out your essay. Use the scratch paper provided to jot down a quick outline of the points you intend to make. Then spend about 25 minutes writing the essay. This should be plenty of time; remember that you're only looking at three or four paragraphs at the most. This schedule will leave about three to five minutes at the end to proofread your essay for spelling and grammar.

STAY WITHIN THE LINES!

Make sure you write your essay only in the lined area provided on the Writing Sample Response Form. That is the only area that will be scanned and sent to law schools. If you write outside of the area provided, your essay will not be reproduced in full.

KAPLAN'S FOUR-STEP METHOD FOR THE WRITING SAMPLE

As you know, you have only 35 minutes to complete the Writing Sample, which comes at the end of the LSAT day. You need to show the law school admissions counselors that you can develop a sound argument and express yourself in clearly written English. You might think this will be a tough task since you will undoubtedly be exhausted from the exam. But, if you follow our four-step plan for the LSAT Writing Sample, the task will become much easier.

Use this brief four-step plan as your guide for test day. More detailed descriptions of each step, along with practice exercises, are covered beginning on page 108 in Chapter 3.

1. Prompt

Read the prompt carefully. Before you start to write, be sure you understand the prompt and the scenario it presents. Writing off topic suggests that you are unable to focus your ideas, or that you don't care.

2. Plan

Decide which alternative you will support based on the number and quality of your supporting examples. *It doesn't have to be your real opinion,* but you must express a clear opinion and support it with the types of reasoning you learned in Logical Reasoning. Always plan your approach thoroughly before you start to write. Essays that wander aimlessly, or start with one opinion but change to another halfway through, are unpleasant to read and make an overall bad impression.

3. Produce

Use most of your time to write the essay. Think through each sentence before starting to write it. Start a new paragraph for each new idea. Stick to your plan.

4. Proofread

Don't skip this step. Save a couple of minutes to make sure you haven't left out words (or even sentences) that are necessary for the reader to follow your reasoning. Planning to proofread also helps ensure that you will complete the essay.

Now that you have an overview of what is involved in the LSAT Writing Sample, let's move on to a review of basic grammar, mechanics, and style. Brushing up on these skills will help you feel confident on test day so that you can easily compose a sound Writing Sample. The refresher will help you craft your personal statement as well.

Chapter 2: **Essential Writing Skills: Grammar, Mechanics, and Style**

Law school admissions counselors aren't just interested in subjects and topics. They also care about vocabulary and basic writing mechanics. This chapter takes a detailed look at the nuts and bolts of writing, down to the smallest levels—word choice and sentence structure.

Our eight maxims of effective writing cover the essentials of grammar, usage, mechanics, and style—everything from subject-verb agreement to semicolons, from parallel structure to point of view. These are the most important things you need to learn (or review) to help you write a strong LSAT Writing Sample and a dazzling personal statement.

After the essentials, you'll find practice exercises to help you measure how much you've learned and to reinforce what you already know. In fact, the exercises will sometimes include items that do not have any mistakes! So stay on your toes and keep your skills sharp.

EIGHT MAXIMS OF EFFECTIVE WRITING

There are dozens and dozens of writing rules and guidelines, and it can be easy to feel overwhelmed by them, especially when you're under pressure to prepare for an exam or see a deadline looming for your law school application. To help you remember what's most important and feel more in control, we've organized those rules and guidelines around eight maxims of effective writing. Use these eight principles as your guide as you prepare for the LSAT Writing Sample and your personal statement.

MAXIM 1: BE CORRECT

Your essays will be easier to understand and, thus, more persuasive, if you follow the conventions of Standard Written English. This section covers the most important rules of grammar, usage, and mechanics as well as the most frequently confused words.

Grammar and Usage

A few grammar errors won't detract from the argument in your Writing Sample. They also won't send your application into the decline pile, but grammatical errors in your personal statement can be more damaging. After all, admissions officers know you only have 35 minutes to write your LSAT Writing Sample, but months to craft a winning personal statement.

Verb Forms and Tenses

Certain types of errors are more likely to strike your readers as more egregious than others. Verb mistakes are among the most damaging, so here's a detailed review of common kinds of errors.

Helping Verbs   Helping or auxiliary verbs do just that: they help you express exactly when an event will or did take place (e.g., future, past perfect, and conditional tenses). They also convey very specific meanings.

Though we often use them interchangeably, *may* and *can* actually have two different meanings. *May* expresses permission, while *can* expresses ability. Thus the question May I? is actually very different from the question Can I?

Here's a list of specific helping verb meanings:

can/could	ability	A radio ad <u>could</u> really expand our customer base.
may/might	permission	You <u>may</u> see the director now.
	possibility	We <u>may</u> benefit considerably from a radio ad.
should	expectation	We <u>should</u> have the results of the survey by Friday.
	recommendation	You <u>should</u> conduct a customer satisfaction survey.
must (have/had)	necessity	We <u>must have</u> the survey results by Friday.
will/shall/would	intention	We <u>shall</u> deliver the survey results by Friday.

Troublesome Verbs   Time to review those three sets of verbs that tend to give writers so much trouble: *lie/lay, rise/raise,* and *sit/set.*

The key to choosing the right word is to remember which verb in each pair is **transitive** and which is **intransitive**. A transitive verb needs an object to receive its action (you can think of it as <u>trans</u>ferring its action to the object). An intransitive verb does not take an object; it performs the action on itself.

Intransitive (no object)		**Transitive** (takes an object)	
lie	to rest or recline	**lay**	to put or place (something)
rise	to go up	**raise**	to lift or move (something) up
sit	to rest	**set**	to put place (something)

> A pneumonic trick to remember which verbs are *i*ntransitive: The first vowel in each word is *i.*

After hours of negotiating, Barker had to <u>lie</u> down and take a nap.

After hours of negotiating, Barker <u>lay</u> his <u>head</u> upon the table and fell asleep.

Nolan likes to <u>rise</u> at 4:30 so he can work for several hours before breakfast.

The Federal Reserve <u>raised</u> the <u>interest</u> <u>rate</u> for the third time this quarter.

Justine is going to <u>sit</u> in the back of the room and observe the training class.

I've <u>set</u> <u>everything</u> you'll need for the conference call on your desk.

Subjunctive and Conditional   The subjunctive voice is actually a simple form but one that has been slipping out of everyday usage over the last several decades. However, it is still required for grammatically correct sentences. The subjunctive is primarily used to express something that is wished for or contrary to fact. To form the subjunctive, use the base form of the verb for all persons and numbers. The only exception is also the most frequently used subjunctive verb, *to be*. The subjunctive of *to be* is *were*:

If I <u>were</u> in your position, I would ask for a second opinion.

The mayor wishes [or wished] that the commercial tax base <u>were</u> larger.

Phrases such as *it is* (or any other tense of the verb *to be*) *necessary that . . .* also take the subjunctive form. Other adjectives and adjectival phrases that may be used in this expression include *vital, essential, indispensable, preferable, advisable, just as well, better,* and *best.*

CORRECT: It is essential that the President <u>recognize</u> the limits of his mandate.

CORRECT: It would be better for all concerned that the patient <u>be</u> informed of his condition.

CORRECT: Is it really necessary that we all <u>study</u> the law in order to protect ourselves from nuisance lawsuits?

CORRECT: The CEO <u>suggested that</u> the secretary <u>revise</u> the report before releasing it.

WATCH OUT FOR WOULD!

A conditional sentence does not normally have *would* in the *if clause*. The exception is when *would* means *be willing to*, as in *If you would dry the dishes, I'll wash them*. In most cases, *would* or *would have* in the *if clause* is wrong:

> INCORRECT: If the town would have raised taxes, it wouldn't have gone bankrupt.

> CORRECT: If the town had raised taxes, it wouldn't have gone bankrupt.

> INCORRECT: If we would have been more prepared, we would have landed the account.

> CORRECT: If we had been more prepared, we would have landed the account.

Practice 1

Find and correct the mistake(s) in the following sentences. Answers are found on page 75.

1. Most of us wish that our parents will be better prepared to face retirement.

   _____

   _____

   _____

2. While we may wish that our physical conditioning would be better, few of us are prepared to invest the time and effort in the kind of exercise and diet that might help us achieve it.

   _____

   _____

   _____

3. Does it make sense to wish that we were armed with lethal claws and teeth like other animals?

   _____

   _____

   _____

4. Although it is easy to mouth words of support for the work of other people, it is preferable that they be given negative feedback where it applies.

   _____

   _____

   _____

5. Many scientists recommend that the government make an effort to preserve every species.

   _____

   _____

   _____

6. Judging from recent pricing patterns, it is imperative that the American government begins to regulate retail milk prices.

   _____

   _____

   _____

Gerunds and Infinitives   Although gerunds look like verbs because they end in *–ing*, they are actually nouns:

> Kinsley's organization promotes awareness of global <u>warming</u>.

Infinitives are formed by combining *to* + the verb base: *to warm*.

The main mistake people make with gerunds and infinitives is using the wrong form after a conjugated verb. Fortunately, if you are a native speaker of English, you can usually hear right away when this kind of error is made:

> INCORRECT: Kinsley hopes <u>promoting</u> awareness of global warming.
>
> CORRECT: Kinsley hopes <u>to promote</u> awareness of global warming.

For some verbs, either a gerund or infinitive will do, though sometimes one sounds a little better than the other:

> CORRECT: Kinsley's goal is <u>to promote</u> awareness of global warming.
>
> *(Best choice)*
>
> CORRECT: Kinsley's goal is <u>promoting</u> awareness of global warming.
>
> *(Also correct)*

The verbs *like, hate,* and other words that express preference fall into this either/or category. But many verbs can only take one form. Here are some general guidelines for when to use infinitives and gerunds.

Gerunds should always follow prepositions and the following verbs:

admit	keep
appreciate	miss
avoid	postpone
cannot help	practice
consider	put off
delay	quit
deny	recall
discuss	recommend
dislike	resist
enjoy	risk
escape	suggest
finish	tolerate
imagine	

Infinitives generally follow these verbs, even when separated by a noun or pronoun:

- advise (I <u>advise</u> you <u>to go</u> to graduate school)

- agree (We <u>agree</u> <u>to stop</u> fighting.)

- allow (Please <u>allow</u> us <u>to present</u> you with this award for your service to the community.)

- ask (They have <u>asked</u> us <u>to write</u> a proposal for developing the Tulman Park area.)

beg	encourage
bother	expect
cause	fail
claim	force
command	hope
convince	manage
decide	need
offer	require
order	tell
persuade	urge
plan	venture
pretend	want
promise	warn
refuse	wish
remind	

CORRECT: The CEO <u>advised</u> the stockholders not <u>to sell</u> before reading the latest report.

CORRECT: The CEO <u>recommended</u> <u>waiting</u> for the quarterly report before making a decision.

Subject-Verb Agreement

Is it "he go" or "he goes"? Native speakers of English can generally count on their inner ear to pick the right form without any conscious thought. But in long, complex sentences or sentences with indefinite pronouns, even native speakers can sometimes make mistakes.

First, the rule: Subject-verb agreement means that the subject must agree with (be equal to) the verb in number. A singular subject (*she*) must have a singular verb (*understands*); a plural subject (*they*) must have a plural verb (*understand*).

Here's a review of the most common kinds of subject-verb agreement errors.

Indefinite Pronouns *Every, each, everyone, everybody, anyone,* and *anybody* are all grammatically singular, even though they tend to have plural meanings.

> INCORRECT: Each of us <u>have</u> completed a review of our department.

> CORRECT: Each of us <u>has</u> completed a review of our department.

> INCORRECT: Anyone who <u>attempt</u> to change my mind will only be disappointed.

> CORRECT: Anyone who <u>attempts</u> to change my mind will only be disappointed.

With these expressions there are often problems of pronoun-antecedent agreement as well as issues of political correctness when you need a singular pronoun to refer to both men and women. You might want to avoid them altogether and use *all* instead:

> INCORRECT: <u>Every</u> one of the delegates has cast <u>their</u> vote.

> CORRECT: <u>Every</u> one of the delegates has cast <u>his or her</u> vote.

> CORRECT: <u>All</u> of the delegates have cast <u>their</u> votes.

Practice 2

The following sentences contain various problem areas in subject-verb agreement. From the two choices provided, choose the verb form that matches the subject of the sentence. Answers are found on page 75.

1. Many people in New York **travel/travels** by subway.

2. Workers in New York often **commute/commutes** a long way to work.

3. Tourists in New York **expect/expects** to see the subway.

4. The "redbird" subway cars with a red body **has/have** been a common sight in New York until recently.

5. The streets of large cities such as New York **is/are** undercut by complex networks of subway tunnels.

6. Today, the economy of New York and other large cities **is/are** booming.

7. New Yorkers with a good income **is/are** less likely to commute by subway.

8. A worker with a long commute **does/do** not want to spend hours on the subway.

9. A private car, although convenient, **pollutes/pollute** the air.

10. Parking in one of New York's many overcrowded garages **is/are** also a problem.

11. Every day, Joe and Carla **rides/ride** the subway to work.

12. Every day, Joe or Carla **rides/ride** the subway to work.

13. Every day, Joe's sisters or Carla's sisters **rides/ride** the subway to work.

14. Every day, Joe's sisters or Carla **rides/ride** the subway to work.

15. Every day, Carla or Joe's sisters from Long Island **rides/ride** the subway to work.

16. Everyone **enjoys/enjoy** a summer vacation.

17. Nobody **has/have** fun when the Cyclones lose a game.

18. Either of the answers **is/are** valid in response to that question.

19. Each of the students **bring/brings** a book to class every day.

20. Many **is/are** obsessed with reality television these days.

Prepositional Distracters   Errors frequently creep in when the grammatical subject of the sentence is singular but includes a prepositional phrase with a plural object. Remember that the object in a prepositional phrase is never the true subject of the sentence. To help you identify this kind of error, read the sentence *without* the prepositional phrase. Correct the error by changing the verb to match the true subject, by moving the prepositional phrase, or by recasting the sentence so that the object of the preposition becomes the true subject. (The prepositional phrases are bracketed in the first two examples below.)

> INCORRECT: The <u>aim</u> [of all promotional strategies] <u>are</u> to influence the shape of the demand curve.

> CORRECT: The <u>aim</u> [of all promotional strategies] <u>is</u> to influence the shape of the demand curve.

> CORRECT: All promotional <u>strategies</u> <u>have</u> the goal of influencing the shape of the demand curve.

> CORRECT: All promotional <u>strategies</u> <u>aim</u> to influence the shape of the demand curve.

When a singular subject is modified by a prepositional phrase that seems to expand the subject, the verb nonetheless agrees only with the true subject.

> CORRECT: The <u>president</u>, along with the vice president and the members of the cabinet, <u>is</u> the highest security risk in times of crisis.

> CORRECT: The <u>president</u> and the <u>vice president</u>, together with the members of the cabinet, <u>are protected</u> by numerous security officers.

Other common expressions that function in a similar way are *besides, as well as, in addition to,* and *not to mention.*

Practice 3

Find and correct the mistake(s) in the following sentences. Answers are found on page 77.

1. The installation of video cameras in public areas certainly add a measure of security but may eventually erode our right to privacy.

2. Competition for grades, jobs, and mates ultimately benefit society.

3. The main flaw in most of these arguments are reliance upon unsupported inferences.

Other Interrupters   Subject-verb agreement errors are also common when the subject and the verb are separated by an intervening adverbial or adjectival phrase.

> INCORRECT: At the national level, each <u>government</u>, regardless of the prevailing economic and political institutions, <u>formulate</u> policies that regulate the international marketing efforts of both domestic and foreign firms.

> CORRECT: At the national level, each <u>government</u>, regardless of the prevailing economic and political institutions, <u>formulates</u> policies that regulate the international marketing efforts of both domestic and foreign firms.

> INCORRECT: The political <u>cartoon</u> depicting the prime minister as a cowboy corralling immigrants <u>have caused</u> a great deal of controversy.

> CORRECT: The political <u>cartoon</u> depicting the prime minister as a cowboy corralling immigrants <u>has caused</u> a great deal of controversy.

Group Nouns   Group or collective nouns refer to a class or group and are almost always treated as singular because they emphasize the group as a single unit or entity. When the context of the sentence makes it clear that the writer is referring to the individual members of the group, then the noun is treated as plural. Group nouns include *audience, class, committee, company, family, firm, government, group, jury, team,* as well as proper names referring to companies and other corporate entities.

> INCORRECT: The research group meet weekly to discuss their progress.

> CORRECT: The research group meets weekly to discuss its progress.

> CORRECT: The members of the research group meet weekly to discuss their progress.

> INCORRECT: The jury is engaged in a heated debate.

> CORRECT: The jury are engaged in a heated debate. [Calls attention to the individual members and their opinions.]

> CORRECT: The members of the jury are engaged in a heated debate.

Be careful with *a number of* and *the number of.* *A number of* means *some* and is plural. *The number* (whether or not it is followed by a prepositional phrase) is singular.

> CORRECT: A <u>number</u> of politicians <u>have</u> urged passage of a Constitutional amendment making same-sex marriage illegal.

> CORRECT: The <u>number</u> of politicians who refuse donations from political action groups <u>is</u> extremely small.

Practice 4

Find and correct the mistake(s) in the following sentences. Answers are found on page 77.

1. The entire team of scientists were allergic to the very chemicals they were studying.

    _____

    _____

    _____

    _____

    _____

    _____

    _____

    _____

2. The research team is scheduled to conclude its work this week.

    _____

    _____

    _____

    _____

    _____

    _____

    _____

3. A number of Internet companies is doubtless preparing to challenge Google for dominance of the search engine market.

    _____

    _____

    _____

    _____

    _____

    _____

    _____

Compound Subjects   First, the easy part: a subject that consists of two or more nouns connected by *and* takes the plural form of the verb.

> CORRECT: The <u>Trash-Site Safety Council</u>, a public interest nonprofit organization, and <u>Eco-Farms International</u>, an association of organic farmers, <u>are monitoring</u> development of upstate landfill projects.

Either/Neither   Now the trickier part. When the subject consists of two or more nouns connected by *or* or *nor*, the verb agrees with the CLOSEST noun.

> CORRECT: Either the senators or <u>the president</u> <u>is</u> misinformed.

> CORRECT: Either the president or the <u>senators</u> <u>are</u> misinformed.

Practice 5

Find and correct the mistake(s) in the following sentences. Answers are found on page 77.

1. The CEO, along with the board of directors, are responsible for any infraction of the corporation's environmental protection policy.

_____

_____

_____

_____

_____

_____

_____

_____

2. Either the attorney general or his senior assistants has the option prosecuting such violations.

_____

_____

_____

_____

_____

_____

_____

3. Neither the professor nor the students have any strong interest in postponing the end of classes.

_____

_____

_____

_____

_____

_____

_____

Pronouns

When you answer the telephone and someone asks for you, do you reply "This is she" or "This is her"? Pronouns are marvelously useful in that they save us from having to repeat the names of people and objects over and over. But there are several kinds of pronoun errors that can plague even seasoned writers.

Pronoun-Antecedent Agreement   Though it may sound right to say "Each delinquent client has now paid their bill in full," the pronoun *their* is incorrect. The subject is singular: *each client*. The verb is also singular: *has*. Thus the pronoun must also be singular to agree with *client*, its **antecedent** (the word a pronoun replaces or refers to):

> CORRECT: Each delinquent <u>client</u> has now paid <u>its</u> bill in full.

Mistakes often occur when the antecedent is an indefinite pronoun. Singular indefinite pronouns include the following:

anybody	everything
anyone	neither
anything	no one
each	nobody
either	somebody
everybody	someone
everyone	something

These are singular antecedents that require singular pronouns:

> INCORRECT: I have asked <u>everyone</u> to write down <u>their</u> preferences for travel accommodations.

> CORRECT: I have asked <u>everyone</u> to write down <u>his or her</u> preferences for travel accommodations.

Plural indefinite pronouns include *both, few, many,* and *several*. They are plural antecedents that require plural pronouns:

> INCORRECT: I have carefully considered your offers, and <u>both</u> are appealing, but <u>it</u> is simply too costly.

> CORRECT: I have carefully considered your offers, and <u>both</u> are appealing, but <u>they</u> are simply too costly.

Some indefinite pronouns—*all, any, most, none,* and *some*—can be either singular or plural depending upon the noun or pronoun to which the indefinite pronoun refers. Here are some examples (notice also how the verbs change to agree with the subjects):

> SINGULAR: Does <u>any owner</u> still have <u>his or her</u> original deed?

> PLURAL: Do <u>any</u> of the <u>owners</u> still have <u>their</u> original deeds?

> SINGULAR: <u>None</u> of the <u>waste product</u> can be recycled, so <u>it</u> must be stored in an airtight container and placed in underground storage.

> PLURAL: <u>None</u> of the <u>waste products</u> can be recycled, so <u>they</u> must be stored in airtight containers and placed in underground storage.

KAPLAN

Correct Pronoun Case So what's the correct response when someone asks for you on the telephone? Answer: "This is <u>he</u>" or "This is <u>she</u>" or "It is <u>I</u>." Why? Because in this situation the pronoun is functioning as a subject and must be in the subjective case.

	Subjective case	Objective case
singular	I	me
	you	you
	he/she/it	him/her/it
plural	we	us
	you	you
	they	them
relative pronoun	who	whom

Whenever the pronoun functions as a subject, use the subjective case. Whenever the pronoun functions as an object, use the objective case. Remember that pronouns in prepositional phrases are *always* objects.

INCORRECT: William promised to keep the content of our conversation between <u>he</u> and <u>I</u>.

CORRECT: William promised to keep the content of our conversation between <u>him</u> and <u>me</u>.

INCORRECT: To <u>who</u> should I address a letter of complaint?

CORRECT: To <u>whom</u> should I address a letter of complaint?

Pronouns in comparative *than* clauses are always subjects because a verb always follows the pronoun, even if that verb is only implied:

INCORRECT: We have been in business much longer than <u>him</u>.

CORRECT: We have been in business much longer than <u>he</u>.

The second version is correct because the sentence includes an unstated but understood verb at the end: *We have been in business much longer than <u>he</u> has.* Here's another example:

INCORRECT: The Jensens are more likely to get the contract than <u>us</u> because they have more up-to-date equipment.

CORRECT: The Jensens are more likely to get the contract than <u>we</u> [are] because they have more up-to-date equipment.

Other Pronoun Issues Finally, two last comments about pronouns.

1. Don't forget that **possessive pronouns do not use an apostrophe**. *Your* is a pronoun; *you're* is a contraction of *you are*.

   INCORRECT: When potential customers cancel <u>they're</u> orders, we need to carefully evaluate <u>they're</u> reasons for cancellation.

   CORRECT: When potential customers cancel <u>their</u> orders, we need to carefully evaluate <u>their</u> reasons for cancellation.

2. The relative pronouns **who/whom, that**, and **which** are often misused. Here are the guidelines:

   Use *who/whom* when referring to people.

   > INCORRECT: Two entrepreneurs <u>which</u> have created multimillion dollar empires and <u>which</u> are under 30 will be the keynote speakers at the seminar.

   > CORRECT: Two entrepreneurs <u>who</u> have created multimillion dollar empires and <u>who</u> are under 30 will be the keynote speakers at the seminar.

Use *that* when referring to things.

> INCORRECT: ABC Candles offers several candle-making classes <u>which</u> are very popular.

> CORRECT: ABC Candles offers several candle-making classes <u>that</u> are very popular.

Use *which* to introduce clauses that provide information that is *not* essential to the sentence. Exception: if the clause refers to people, use *who*.

> INCORRECT: ABC Candles, <u>that</u> is located on Elm Street, offers weekly candle-making classes.

> CORRECT: ABC Candles, <u>which</u> is located on Elm Street, offers weekly candle-making classes.

> [The information *which is located on Elm Street* is not essential to the sentence.]

Modifiers

Modifiers are those words, phrases, and clauses that serve to describe (modify) other words in a sentence. Here's the number one rule regarding modifiers: To keep your sentences clear and correct, always place your modifiers as close as possible to the word(s) they modify.

Misplaced Modifiers   If you violate the proximity rule, you're likely to end up with a misplaced modifier, which is exactly that—a modifier that is in the wrong place. These are usually quite easily corrected by moving the modifying clause or phrase right next to its subject.

> INCORRECT: Satisfied and sleepy after a full bottle of milk, the mother laid her baby in the crib.

> CORRECT: The mother laid her baby, satisfied and sleepy after a full bottle of milk, in the crib.

> INCORRECT: Frightened by the threat of a bear market, the newspaper reported that investors were apprehensive about buying stocks.

> CORRECT: The newspaper reported that investors, frightened by the threat of a bear market, were apprehensive about buying stocks.

Dangling Modifiers   Another common modifier error is the dangling modifier. Here the problem is that the subject of the modifying phrase or clause is different from the subject of the main clause or is simply unclear.

> DANGLER: Having studied countless sick cows, they were placed on a diet of organic feed and antibiotics.

> > [*The subject of the introductory participle* having studied *would have to be scientists, veterinarians, or some other group; but the subject of the main clause,* they, *refers to the cows themselves.*]

> UNDANGLED: Having studied countless sick cows, the veterinarians placed the cows on a diet of organic feed and antibiotics.

Practice 6

Find and correct the mistake(s) in the following sentences. Answers are found on page 77.

1. Looking at the data carefully, the premises simply will not support the conclusion.

    _____

    _____

    _____

    _____

    _____

    _____

    _____

    _____

2. Having selected an appropriate brand name, there are still many obstacles to successful market-
    ing of the new product.

    _____

    _____

    _____

    _____

    _____

    _____

    _____

    _____

3. In this argument, an essential inference is that to pass the course the exam must be taken.

    _____

    _____

    _____

    _____

    _____

    _____

    _____

Adjectives and Adverbs   A few short words about adjectives (which modify nouns and pronouns) and adverbs (which modify verbs, adjectives, and other adverbs) to help prevent some common errors:

1. *Good* is an adjective; *well* is an adverb.

    CORRECT: Irina made several good suggestions for revising the application process.

    CORRECT: The new application process is working very well.

2. Use the adjective *less* to modify singular nouns representing a quantity or degree. Use *fewer* to modify plural nouns or things that can be counted.

    INCORRECT: There are less benefits to outsourcing than we first believed.

    CORRECT: There are fewer benefits to outsourcing than we first believed.

3. The comparative form should be used when comparing two things. The superlative should be used when comparing three or more things.

    Comparative: *-er* or *more/less*

    > *heavier, more innovative*

    Superlative: *-est* or *most/least*

    > *heaviest, most innovative*

4. Don't double up. Only one negative or one comparative is needed.

    INCORRECT: So far we have been more luckier than last year with the weather during our sidewalk sales.

    CORRECT: So far we have been luckier than last year with the weather during our sidewalk sales.

    INCORRECT: We don't have no doubt that our plan will increase business.

    CORRECT: We don't have any doubt that our plan will increase business.

Parallel Structure   An essential element of proper sentence construction is parallel structure, which is really another variation on the idea that items in a sentence should be balanced. Parallelism means that similar elements in a series, list, or two-part construction (e.g., *not only/but also*) should be expressed in parallel grammatical form: all nouns, all infinitives, all gerunds, all prepositional phrases, or all clauses.

> INCORRECT: All business students should learn word processing, accounting, and how to program computers.
>
> CORRECT: All business students should learn word processing, accounting, and computer programming.

The parallelism principle applies to any words that might begin each item in a series: prepositions (in, on, by, with, etc.), articles (*the, a, an*), helping verbs (*had, has, would*, etc.) and possessives (*his, her, our*, etc.). Either repeat the word before every element in a series or include it only before the first item. Anything else violates the rules of parallelism. In effect, your treatment of the second element of the series determines the form of all subsequent elements.

KAPLAN

INCORRECT: He invested his money <u>in</u> stocks, <u>in</u> real estate, and a home for retired performers.

CORRECT: He invested his money <u>in</u> stocks, <u>in</u> real estate, and <u>in</u> a home for retired performers.

CORRECT: He invested his money in stocks, real estate, and a home for retired performers.

When proofreading, check that each item in the series agrees with the word or phrase that begins the series. In the above example, *invested his money* is the common phrase that each item shares. You would read "He *invested his money in real estate, (invested his money) in stocks,* and *(invested his money) in a home for retired performers."* A number of two-part sentence constructions also call for you to always express ideas in parallel form. These constructions include:

X is as _____ as *Y*.

X is more/less _____ than *Y*.

The more/less X, the more/less Y.

Both X and Y . . .

Either X or Y . . .

Neither X nor Y . . .

Not only X but also Y . . .

X and *Y* can stand for as little as one word or as much as a whole clause, but in any case the grammatical structure of *X* and *Y* must be identical.

INCORRECT: The downturn in sales was attributed not only to <u>the recession</u> but also <u>because</u> a new competitor entered the market.

CORRECT: The downturn in sales was attributed not only to <u>the recession</u> but also to the entrance of a new competitor into the market.

INCORRECT: Generally, <u>the profits from sales of</u> everyday necessities are not nearly as spectacular <u>as from</u> luxury items.

CORRECT: Generally, <u>the profits from sales of</u> everyday necessities are not nearly as spectacular as <u>those from the sale of</u> luxury items.

It is often rhetorically effective to use a particular construction several times in succession to emphasize a particular idea or series of thoughts. The technique is called parallel construction, and it is effective only when used sparingly because it works on a larger (multiple-sentence) scale. Here's how parallel construction should be used:

CORRECT PARALLELISM: As a leader, Lincoln inspired a nation to throw off the chains of slavery; as a philosopher, he proclaimed the greatness of the little man; as a human being, he served as a timeless example of humility.

The repetition of the sentence structure (*As a X, Lincoln Y...*) provides a strong sense of rhythm and organization to the sentence and alerts the reader to yet another aspect of Lincoln's character. However, careless writers sometimes use a parallel structure for expressions of *dissimilar* structure.

INCORRECT: They are sturdy, attractive, and cost only a dollar each.

[The phrase *They are* makes sense preceding the adjectives *sturdy* and *attractive,* but cannot be understood before *cost only a dollar each.*]

CORRECT: They are sturdy and attractive, and they cost only a dollar each.

Practice 7

Find and correct the mistake(s) in the following sentences. Answers are found on page 78.

1. For example, I would say that my roommate could be characterized as a poor student because he waited until the last minute to study for exams, wrote his lab reports without completing the assigned experiments, and his motivation was low.

   _____

   _____

   _____

   _____

   _____

   _____

   _____

2. It is reasonable for a Kravis Software sales representative to expect that he will have an opportunity to introduce his products at the meeting, that there will be a projector for his slide presentation, and prospective buyers will ask questions about the product.

   _____

   _____

   _____

   _____

   _____

   _____

   _____

3. Before investing in a start-up company, the venture capitalist meets with the company's principals, reviews the business plan, and would evaluate samples of the product or service that the company plans to offer.

   _____

   _____

   _____

   _____

   _____

   _____

   _____

Sentence Fragments

In real life, full-blown grammatically complete sentences are a rarity. Most speech takes the form of what would qualify as a "sentence fragment" if it occurred in writing. But in your LSAT Writing Sample and your personal statement, you'll want to write only in complete sentences.

What exactly is a fragment? An incomplete sentence (like this one). To be complete, a sentence must have both a subject and a verb *and* express a complete thought. Often fragments are dependent clauses that need another sentence to make a complete thought:

> FRAGMENT: <u>While we are reorganizing the department</u>. Harrison will be the interim office manager.
>
> > [*The first sentence is a dependent clause that cannot stand alone;* while *makes it depend upon the second sentence.*]

These fragments have an easy fix: simply combine the dependent and independent clauses into one sentence.

> COMPLETE THOUGHT: While we are reorganizing the <u>department, Harrison</u> will be the interim office manager.

Other times a fragment is a clause or phrase missing a subject or verb, or both. The solution: add the missing subject or verb, or attach the loose clause or phrase to the core sentence.

> FRAGMENT: Cheyenne has been researching ways to conserve energy. <u>Without sacrificing production</u>.
>
> COMPLETE THOUGHT: Cheyenne has been researching ways to conserve <u>energy without</u> sacrificing production.

Sometimes a relative pronoun (*that, who, which*) causes the fragment, which can be corrected by simply deleting the pronoun.

> FRAGMENT: Cheyenne, <u>who</u> has been researching ways to conserve energy without sacrificing production.
>
> COMPLETE THOUGHT: Cheyenne has been researching ways to conserve energy without sacrificing production.

Practice 8

Some of the sentences in the following short passage are sentence fragments. Identify the fragments and fix them by adding or removing the necessary words to make complete sentences. Answers are found on page 78.

Everyone feels shy. At some point in life. It is perfectly normal to be concerned about how strangers might view you in an unfamiliar situation. For example, a social gathering or new job. However, shyness can sometimes become a major difficulty. If a person feels overpowering anxiety about common situations such as going to the store, attending classes at school or even walking down the street. That anxiety can interfere with the person's ability to carry on a normal life. A few shy people develop a serious fear of strangers. Forcing them to restrict or avoid contact with people most of us interact with daily. Such as the mail carrier, co-workers, or teachers. These people who feel overwhelmed by the mere thought of contact with a stranger. Such people may have agoraphobia.

_____

_____

_____

_____

_____

_____

_____

_____

_____

_____

_____

_____

_____

_____

_____

_____

_____

_____

_____

_____

Run-on Sentences

Run-ons are sentences that literally run right into each other because sometimes there is a comma between them but a comma alone is not strong enough to separate two complete thoughts.

Okay, let's try that again: Run-ons are sentences that literally run right into each other. Sometimes there is a comma between them; however, a comma alone is not strong enough to separate two complete thoughts.

There are four ways to correct run-on sentences:

1. Separate the sentences with a period.

    INCORRECT: Cheyenne has been researching ways to conserve <u>energy, she</u> will submit her findings by Friday.

    CORRECT: Cheyenne has been researching ways to conserve <u>energy. She</u> will submit her findings by Friday.

2. Separate them with a comma *and* a coordinating conjunction (*and, or, for, nor, but, so* and *yet*).

    CORRECT: Cheyenne wants to conserve energy<u>, but</u> she is worried about sacrificing production.

3. Separate them with a semicolon. Use this option when the two ideas are closely related.

    CORRECT: Cheyenne has been researching ways to conserve <u>energy; she</u> is also seeking more eco-friendly suppliers.

4. Make one sentence dependent upon the other by adding a subordinating conjunction such as *since, because, while, although, during,* and *before*.

    CORRECT: <u>Although it might mean slightly increased costs,</u> Cheyenne wants to use more eco-friendly suppliers.

It is also correct to separate the two sentences with a dash, but *only* if you wish to set the second sentence off for emphasis.

    CORRECT: Cheyenne wants to conserve energy—but only if it doesn't sacrifice production.

Note: *However* is not a subordinating conjunction; it is a conjunctive adverb. Use it with a semicolon, not a comma, to join two independent clauses.

    CORRECT: Cheyenne wants to conserve energy; however, she is worried about sacrificing production.

Mechanics

Mechanics refers to the rules for punctuation, capitalization, and spelling. These types of mistakes are easy for your reader to recognize, whether they are reading your essay closely or not, so you should pay extra attention to using proper mechanics.

Punctuation

Comma   If you are a writer who finds comma rules confusing, you're in a bit of luck. Let's review the places where you *do* need a comma:

- To set off **appositive** or **nonrestrictive material** within the sentence—that is, information that is relevant but not essential to the core sentence. (Obviously, if the material occurs at the beginning or the end of the sentence, only one comma will be needed.)

   CORRECT: Early retirement was offered to 11 employees, all of whom have been employed for over 25 years.

   CORRECT: Dwayne, who has been an employee for over 25 years, has accepted the offer of early retirement.

- To set off **transitional expressions**, **interjections**, or **nouns of direct address**:

   CORRECT: Critics of the proposal, however, will doubtless focus on the unknown risks.

   CORRECT: Nevertheless, the proponents of the proposal will surely prevail.

   CORRECT: After we review your proposal, Mrs. Jenkins, we'll let you know our decision.

- To separate direct discourse from the speaker or source (unless the quoted phrase is very short):

   CORRECT: I wonder, How can politicians fairly represent such a diverse constituency?

   CORRECT: My supervisor informed me, with a straight face, "Your performance is too good for this department. You're making the rest of us look bad."

   Note that quotation marks are only necessary for direct quotation of an utterance. Otherwise, they are not necessary:

   CORRECT: The question is, Do we need more students?

- Before a **coordinating conjunction** joining two independent clauses.

   CORRECT: It was Kendra's first time interviewing a potential employee, and she was more nervous than the applicant.

- After a long **introductory phrase or clause**.

   CORRECT: Against the advice of his accountant, Auggie did not pay estimated taxes.

- **Between two modifiers** that both modify the same word.

   CORRECT: Hani is a perfect example of a self-educated, highly successful entrepreneur. [Both *self-educated* and *highly successful* modify *entrepreneur*.]

- **Between items in a series**. Again, the comma before the *and* and last item is optional.

   CORRECT: To furnish her new office, Anna bought two filing cabinets, a spacious oak desk, a matching swivel chair, and several framed Ansel Adams photographs.

- Anywhere else it's needed **to prevent confusion**.

   CORRECT: When you think about it, it isn't really all that complicated.

KAPLAN

Now, here are some cases where the comma is superfluous:

- When a direct quotation ends in a question mark or an exclamation point but the sentence continues on, the comma must be omitted:

    INCORRECT: "Millions for defense, but not one cent for tribute!," the newspapers proclaimed.

    CORRECT: "Millions for defense, but not one cent for tribute!" the newspapers proclaimed.

- After very short introductory adverbial expressions if there is no danger of confusion:

    INCORRECT: Every winter, the number of fatal traffic accidents increases due to adverse driving conditions.

    CORRECT: Every winter the number of fatal traffic accidents increases due to adverse driving conditions.

- Around restrictive (essential) phrases

    INCORRECT: Teachers and principals, in the public school system, have been lobbying for more funding for the arts.

    CORRECT: Teachers and principals in the public school system have been lobbying for more funding for the arts.

- Before words quoted indirectly

    INCORRECT: The Supreme Court has ruled that, no evidence gathered by illegal surveillance methods entered into the trial record.

    CORRECT: The Supreme Court has ruled that no evidence gathered by illegal surveillance methods entered into the trial record.

- *After* a coordinating conjunction

    INCORRECT: Every nation must take measures to protect itself from terrorist attacks, but, the rights of citizens to due privacy and equal protection under the law must be protected.

    CORRECT: Every nation must take measures to protect itself from terrorist attacks, but the rights of citizens to due privacy and equal protection under the law must be protected.

Period How and when to use a period may seem straightforward, but especially when it comes to quotations and abbreviations, there are specific rules you need to follow.

- An indirect question embedded within a declarative sentence ends with a period, not a question mark.

    INCORRECT: We must consider why white-collar crime has risen so rapidly?

    CORRECT: We must consider why white-collar crime has risen so rapidly.

- Only one period should appear at the end of a sentence, even if the sentence ends in an abbreviation or a directly quoted sentence. Likewise, a period cannot be combined with a question mark or exclamation mark.

INCORRECT: Investigators recently reported, "The mysterious pollutants have been traced to the Trenton-based Kwalitee Products, Inc.".

INCORRECT: Investigators recently reported, "The mysterious pollutants have been traced to the Trenton-based Kwalitee Products, Inc."

CORRECT: Investigators recently reported, "The mysterious pollutants have been traced to the Trenton-based Kwalitee Products, Inc."

INCORRECT: Connor's brief fax consisted of only one word: "Help!".

CORRECT: Connor's brief fax consisted of only one word: "Help!"

- In abbreviations, no space follows internal periods. Where initials are used instead of names, the general practice is to leave internal spaces, although newspapers do not do so. If initials replace a name, the periods and spaces may be omitted. Whichever style you choose, be consistent.

  INCORRECT: Many students feel that having the letters "Ph. D." after their name will make them more competitive on the job market.

  CORRECT: Many students feel that having the letters "Ph.D." after their name will make them more competitive on the job market.

  INCORRECT: Since the dissolution of the U. S. S. R., political instability has replaced political repression.

  CORRECT: Since the dissolution of the U.S.S.R., political instability has replaced political repression.

- Periods are omitted from acronyms, words formed from the initial letters of a multiword name: NATO (North Atlantic Treaty Organization), GOP (Grand Old Party, i.e. Republican Party), CEO (chief executive officer), etc. Many abbreviated company names are treated as acronyms: IBM, AOL, GM.

- When a quoted phrase appears at the end of a sentence, the period is placed within the quotation marks, even when it did not appear in the original text that is being quoted. (This is the American practice; the British practice is to place the period outside the quotation marks unless it was actually part of the original text.)

  AMERICAN: The prevailing ethos of our westward expansion is summed up in the phrase "Manifest Destiny."

  BRITISH: The prevailing ethos of our westward expansion is summed up in the phrase "Manifest Destiny".

  Need we insist? It's an American test; use the American convention.

Semicolon   For the most part, you should use a semicolon only where you could also use a period—it is a punctuation mark that belongs primarily between two *independent* clauses. The difference between the semicolon and period is that a semicolon still keeps the two clauses together in one sentence. Thus, use a semicolon instead of a period when the two clauses are closely related and you want to keep a connection between them:

PERIOD: Hillary earned her bachelor's degree in just two and a half years. She then went on to become a teacher of gifted children.

[*These two sentences are sequential, but not closely related.*]

SEMICOLON: Hillary earned her bachelor's degree in just two and a half years; she earned her master's in less than one.

[*These two sentences are closely related; they both deal with Hillary's speed in earning her degrees.*]

The other time to use a semicolon is when one or more items in a list contain an internal comma. In this case you can avoid confusion by using semicolons instead of commas to separate the elements in the list.

CORRECT: Similar incidents have occurred in Houston, Texas; Nashville, Tennessee; and Davis, California.

Practice 9

Find and mark up the mistake(s) in the following sentences. Answers are found on page 79.

1. Elementary schools must impart the tools necessary, to teach the basic skills.

2. The role, of providing lifelong assistance to disabled people, belongs to the government which can muster the vast resources needed to properly care for the ill.

3. Advocates of the proposed law however, will most likely insist on the need to forestall improper sharing of intellectual property, and classified information.

4. All the support for this argument is either flawed superfluous or irrelevant.

5. In fact it is just as likely that some other cause can explain why the products at the uptown factory are cheaper to produce.

6. Although discounted the evidence of the second survey is actually more informative to this argument.

Practice 10

Find and mark up the mistake(s) in the following sentences. Answers are found on page 79.

1. We may well ask ourselves what colleges can possibly do to prevent cheating?

2. Does it actually make sense to ask whether people's lives are more meaningful now than 100 years ago?

3. For years, the largest contingents of international peacekeepers have come from the U. K. and the U. S. A.

Practice 11

Find and mark up the mistake(s) in the following sentences. Answers are found on page 80.

1. When a society is in agreement on the need to meet social objectives, government generally takes on a powerful role, in such cases, levying taxes, rather than simply raising money, becomes, in addition, a means of implementing those goals.

2. The assets of such an enterprise might include, for example, $30 million in real estate, equipment, and infrastructure, $20 million in cash, investments, and accounts receivable, and $10 million in inventory.

3. Many of the food products marketed by McBurger are notoriously high in cholesterol, fat, and calories; the company's sales are therefore likely to decline over the next few years if new product lines are not introduced.

Colon   Less frequently used than commas and semicolons, but no less important, is the colon. The colon has three specific functions. Use a colon:

1.   To introduce a list of three or more items if the list comes *after* an independent clause:

     INCORRECT: Some of the benefits of the new system <u>include: speed</u>, accuracy, and significant savings.

     CORRECT: Some of the benefits of the new system <u>include speed</u>, accuracy, and significant savings

     CORRECT: There are three benefits of the new <u>system: speed</u>, accuracy, and significant savings.

2.   To introduce a quotation if it comes *after* an independent clause:

     INCORRECT: As Thomas Edison said: "Genius is 1% inspiration and 99% perspiration."

     CORRECT: I agree 100% with Thomas Edison: "Genius is 1% inspiration and 99% perspiration."

3.   To introduce an explanation or summary of an independent clause:

     CORRECT: There is one essential ingredient of success, and only one: perseverance.

     CORRECT: The pitch was a complete failure: the client rejected every item in the proposal.

Do **not** use a colon after *such as, for example,* or *including*:

     INCORRECT: The new system offers many benefits, <u>such as: speed</u>, accuracy, and significant savings.

Hyphen and Dash   Often confused because they look alike, the hyphen (-) and the dash (–) perform very different functions. Use a **hyphen** to connect two or more words that work together as one object or modifier:

     CORRECT: The <u>editor-in-chief</u> occasionally does restaurant reviews.

     CORRECT: Our new partnership is clearly a <u>win-win</u> situation.

Use a **dash** to set off a word, phrase or clause for emphasis:

     CORRECT: Pickering—who is just 26 years old—is the youngest CEO of a major corporation.

Question Mark   Use question marks only to indicate a *direct* question is being asked.

     INCORRECT: We often wonder where the time has gone?

     CORRECT: We often wonder, where has the time gone?

Do not place a question mark at the end of an indirect question unless the indirect question itself is embedded in a question.

     INCORRECT: A good leader should always ask herself who will follow her lead?

     CORRECT: A good leader should always ask herself who will follow her lead.

     CORRECT: Should a good leader always ask herself who will follow her lead?

Quotation Marks   Quotation marks enclose text that is a direct quote. They can also be used to indicate a word is being used as a word.

> INCORRECT: This building is zoned for residential office use, the realtor said.
>
> CORRECT: "This building is zoned for residential office use," the realtor said.
>
> CORRECT: The realtor said this building is zoned for residential office use.
>
> INCORRECT: He used the term proactive five times in his introduction.
>
> CORRECT: He used the term "proactive" five times in his introduction.

Here are a few important notes about quotation marks:

- In American usage, commas and periods should be placed <u>inside</u> quotation marks, even when they are not properly part of the quoted material.

  CORRECT: J. D. Salinger's *Catcher in the Rye*, a novel taught in American high schools for generations, caused a fundamental shift in attitudes toward "dirty language."

  CORRECT: "Ask not what your country can do for you," urged the president. "Ask what you can do for your country."

- Colons and semicolons, on the other hand, should *follow* the closing quotation mark.

  CORRECT: I was not one who believed "my country right or wrong"; in fact, having come to age during the Viet Nam War, I tended to assume that our foreign policy was devoid of moral principle.

- Question marks and exclamation marks should be placed <u>inside</u> the quotation marks when they are part of the quoted material and <u>outside</u> when they are not. When a question ends with a quotation that is itself a question, there will be only one question mark: the one inside the quotation marks.

  INCORRECT: Doesn't the judge usually ask the jurors, "Have you reached a verdict?"?

  CORRECT: Doesn't the judge usually ask the jurors, "Have you reached a verdict?"

  CORRECT: The judge asked the jurors, "Have you reached a verdict?"

Apostrophe   The apostrophe is used to form most possessives and contractions, in addition to a few plurals (see above). Here are a few reminders to help you avoid apostrophe errors.

- The apostrophe is used to show *possession*, not *plurality*:

  INCORRECT: Americans eat million's of hamburger's everyday.

  CORRECT: Americans eat millions of hamburgers every day.

- When adding a possessive apostrophe to a plural noun ending in *s*, place the apostrophe after the plural *s* and *omit* the possessives.

  INCORRECT: As new products are developed, the manager must devote some thought to those product's names.

  INCORRECT: As new products are developed, the manager must devote some thought to those products's names.

  CORRECT: As new products are developed, the manager must devote some thought to those products' names.

- If the plural does *not* end in *s*, the possessive is formed, as usual, by adding apostrophe and then *s*.

  INCORRECT: Some peoples' idea of a sacrifice is not watching TV for one evening.

  CORRECT: Some people's idea of a sacrifice is not watching TV for one evening.

- If a singular noun ends in *s*, show possession by adding *'s*.

  INCORRECT: Travis relied on Lukas' expertise to negotiate a fair contract.

  INCORRECT: Travis relied on Luka's expertise to negotiate a fair contract.

  CORRECT: Travis relied on Lukas's expertise to negotiate a fair contract.

- Remember that possessive pronouns do *not* take an apostrophe:

  INCORRECT: The decision is our's [your's, her's, their's].

  CORRECT: The decision is ours [yours, hers, theirs].

The normal way to change a singular noun to plural is by adding *s* or *es*. But when it comes to numbers or other characters, the plural is usually formed by adding *'s*:

CORRECT: How many i's are there in the word *Mississippi*?

CORRECT: A valid email address cannot have two @'s.

Decades have traditionally been accorded apostrophes (e.g., 2000's). These days, however, it is becoming more common to omit the apostrophe (2000s), especially in the abbreviated form, which already uses an apostrophe to indicate the omission of the first two digits of the year:

CORRECT: Having grown up in the 1990s, I believe that world peace is an achievable goal.

UNACCEPTABLE: The '60's and '70's were years of turbulence in many countries.

ACCEPTABLE: The '60s and '70s were years of turbulence in many countries.

ACCEPTABLE: The sixties and seventies were years of turbulence in many countries.

Practice 12

Find and mark up the mistake(s) in the following sentences. Answers are found on page 80.

1. The prompt poses a simple question: The 55 mph limit should be restored?

2. The question posed is, whether the 55 mph limit should be restored.

3. Is there an answer to the question of the feasibility of restoring the 55 mph speed limit?

Practice 13

Find and mark up the mistake(s) in the following sentences. Answers are found on page 80.

1. Three principle's are at issue in this case.

2. Ultimately, a leader must be guided by her peoples wishes.

3. With very few exceptions, womens' rights have been adjudicated by the courts over the past few decade's.

4. Many Prince's of Wales' have served long terms as the heir to the crown of Great Britain, and Prince Charles' case is no exception.

Practice 14

Find the mistake(s) in the following sentences. Answers are found on page 80.

1. In most developing country's, up to 80 percent of the population lives in rural community's.

2. Republicans and Democrats alike may feel uncomfortable about running on their parties' platforms.

3. Human's are not the only primate's that have been known to murder their own kind: infanticide is well-documented among chimpanzee's, baboon's, and several species of monkeys.

Slash   The forward slash (/) has many uses.

- It can mean per, as in m^3/sec (cubic meters per second).

- It can mean and, as in w/d (washer and dryer).

- It can indicate abbreviation, as in w/ and w/o (with and without).

In a nontechnical academic essay such as the LSAT Writing Sample or your personal statement, you should avoid these informal or technical uses of the slash.

One other use of the slash is worth avoiding. Apparently, due to the popularization of *s/he* (read *he or she*) and other attempts to remedy the lack of a gender-neutral singular pronoun in English, the slash has in recent years been tossed around as a short form of *or*. This practice is not likely to gain acceptance in professional or academic prose any more than the use of *&* to replace *and.* Either spell out *or*, or let a single option suffice.

> UNACCEPTABLE: A successful leader will convince/coerce his/her followers to lay aside their hostilities and focus on the challenges facing the community.

> ACCEPTABLE: A successful leader will convince her followers to lay aside their hostilities and focus on the challenges facing the community.

Practice 15

Find the mistake(s) in the following sentences. Answers are found on page 81.

1. In the age of electronic media, reading books/magazines is not as important as it once was.

2. Consumers must have the confidence that they have an option to get a refund/exchange any online purchase that does not meet with their satisfaction.

3. Statistics for births/year/person can give a useful measure of a nation's reproductive status.

Practice 16

The following paragraph contains numerous errors in punctuation. Correct the errors and check your answers against the revised version found on page 81.

(1) Abraham Lincoln described the U.S. government as being as he said in the Gettysburg Address "of the people by the people and for the people." (2) This notion I believe puts the priorities' between the achievements of institutions, and the achievements of governments, in proper perspective. (3) It is not a question, of the achievements of individuals v. s. the achievements of the government, that individual/government contrast is a false dilemma. (4) Rather it is the achievements of individuals which make up the achievements of a government that determine the greatness of a nation. (5) This is what Lincoln meant when he referred to the nations "unfinished work:" that each of us has a task to perform and those tasks determine what kind of nation we will live in. (6) With this fundamental argument in mind how can we not join with Lincoln in wishing that such a nation, "shall not perish from the earth"?

Capitalization

Capitalization is not rocket science, but it is easy to make simple errors. These are the most important points to review.

First, the general principle is this: Capitalize proper nouns—the <u>specific</u> names of people, places, and things. Do not capitalize general items.

Specific	General
Souderton High School	my high school
Aunt Bettie	your favorite aunt
A-Plus Computer Services	computer repair company

Now some more specific guidelines. You should always **capitalize** the following:

- The first word in a sentence

- People's names, as well as titles when used with the name (Judge Blackwell) or, in the case of high officials, when used to refer to a particular person
  CORRECT: In the face of enormous resistance to his foreign policy, President Johnson announced that he would not run for re-election in 1968.
  CORRECT: The president called a press conference to announce his decision.
  CORRECT: The president of the United States is not chosen directly by the people.

- Names of places (but not "the" or "of," unless they fall at the beginning of a sentence), as well as adjectives derived from place names
  CORRECT: The Library of Congress contains several exhibitions in its online gallery.
  CORRECT: There are several exhibitions in the Library of Congress's online gallery.

- Names of institutions (except, again, "the" or "of" and other minor words, unless they fall at the beginning of a sentence)
  CORRECT: I received my letter of acceptance from the University of Pennsylvania today.
  CORRECT: The University of Pennsylvania campus is just five miles from my home.

- Special events and periods (names of holidays, historical events, eras), but not centuries
  CORRECT: The exhibit includes drawings and letters from the historic Battle of the Bulge.

- Names of countries, languages, and religions, and adjectives derived from them
  CORRECT: In the tiny country of Bhutan, nearly every citizen is a Buddhist.

- The stars, planets, and other celestial bodies and structures (the Milky Way, the Crab Nebula)

- The first and all important words of publication titles, movies, songs, works of art
  CORRECT: The television comedy "The Office," like the comic strip "Dilbert," satirizes life behind the cubicle.

Do NOT capitalize the following:

- Any word simply for emphasis
  INCORRECT: The two essential characteristics of any leader are Decisiveness and Communication Skills.
  CORRECT: The two essential characteristics of any leader are decisiveness and communication skills.

- The names of academic subjects, except when referring to the name of a particular course or to a department
  INCORRECT: I plan to major in Anthropology and minor in French Literature.
  CORRECT: I plan to major in anthropology and minor in French literature.
  INCORRECT: This semester I am taking anthropology 101 and introduction to french literature.
  CORRECT: This semester I am taking Anthropology 101 and Introduction to French Literature.

- Seasons

- The first word of a sentence cited in indirect discourse
  INCORRECT: Leah said She was enrolling in the executive MBA program.
  CORRECT: Leah said she was enrolling in the executive MBA program.

Practice 17

Find and mark up the mistake(s) in the following sentences. Answers are found on page 82.

1. During the Middle Ages and most of the Renaissance, Philosophy was hardly distinct from Theology.

2. By the end of Spring, american and canadian University students have been enjoying their Summer Vacation for well over a month.

3. Widely regarded as the most important U. S. Trade Agreement in the past two decades, the U.S.-Canada Free Trade Agreement phased out all tariffs and quotas between the two countries by the end of the Twentieth Century.

4. Last year, doctor sanford was elected president of the brooklyn council. The president of the council meets regularly with the dean of students.

5. american independence day and memorial day occur during the summer, but labor day is in the fall.

6. The novels of william faulkner are set in the american south, and the author himself lived most of his life south of the mason-dixon line.

Frequently Misspelled Words

Most of us could use a good review of these commonly misspelled words—especially those of us who have grown dependent upon the autocorrect feature on our computers.

absence: One *a*, two *e*'s.

accommodate, accommodation: Two *c*'s, two *m*'s

accompany: Two *c*'s.

all right: Two words. *Alright* is *NOT* all right.

a lot: Always two words, never one; do not confuse with *allot*.

argument: No *e* after the *u*.

calendar: *A, e,* then another *a*.

campaign: Remember the *aig* combination.

cannot: Usually spelled as a single word, except where the meaning is "able not to."
> CORRECT: One cannot ignore the importance of conformity.
> CORRECT: Anyone can not pay taxes, but the consequences may be serious.

comparative, comparatively: Yes, *comparison* has an *i* after the *r*. These words don't.

conscience: Spell it with *science*.

correspondent, correspondence: No dance.

definite: Spell it with *finite*, not *finate*.

develop, development: No *e* after the *p*.

embarrass: Two *r*'s, two *s*'s.

every day (adv.): Two words with *every* modifying *day*. Note that there is also an adjective, *everyday,* meaning *commonplace, usual.*
> ADVERB: We see this error *every day*.
> ADJECTIVE: Getting stuck behind an elephant in traffic is no longer an *everyday* occurrence in Katmandu.

exaggerate: One *x*, two *g*'s.

foreign: Think of the *reign* of a *foreign* king.

grammar: No *e*.

KAPLAN

grateful: Spell it with *grate*

harass: One *r*, two *s*'s.

independent, independence: No *dance*.

indispensable: It's something you are not *able* to dispense with.

judgment: No *e* on the end of *judge*.

leisure: Like *pleasure* but with an *i* instead of *a*.

license: In alphabetical order: *c* then *s*, not *lisence*.

maintenance: *main*, then *ten*, then *ance* (reverse alphabetical order for your vowels preceding *n*).

maneuver: Memorize the unusual *eu* combo.

no one: Two words. Don't be mislead by *nobody*, *nothing*, *everyone*, *someone*, and *anyone*.

noticeable: Notice that this one keeps the *e* when adding the suffix.

occur, occurred, occurrence: Double the *r* when you add a suffix beginning with a vowel.

parallel, unparalleled: Two *l*'s, then one.

parenthesis (pl. *parentheses*): Likewise, many other words of Greek origin are spelled with *-is* in the singular and *-es* in the plural; among the more common are *analysis, diagnosis, prognosis, synthesis, thesis.*

perseverance: Only two *r*'s—*sever*, not *server*. Remember that the *a* in the suffix keeps it from being all *e*'s.

professor, professional: One *f*.

pronunciation: Never mind *pronounce* and *pronouncement*: *pronunciation* has no *o* in the second syllable.

questionnaire: Two *n*'s, one *r*.

regardless: Not *irregardless*, an unacceptable yoking of *irrespective* and *regardless*.

responsible, responsibility: While the French and Spanish cognates end in *–able*, it's *–ible* in English.

separate: Look for "a rat" in separate.

unanimous: *un* then *an*.

vacuum: One *c*, two *u*'s.

Doubling Consonants   One of the most confusing issues in spelling is whether to double the final consonant when adding a suffix. *Beginning* or *begining*? *Traveling* or *travelling*? Here's the rule: If the final syllable is accented and the final vowel is short, the consonant is doubled. (Except for *c*, because *c* before *e* or *i* is softened to an *s* sound; we simply add a *k* instead: e.g. *picnic, picnicked*.)

short vowel	
hop	hopped
fat	fatten
set	setting

long vowel	
hope	hoped
fate	fated
seat	seating

There are complications, of course. In American English, this rule only applies if the final syllable of the root word is accented; in British English, it applies whether or not the accent falls on the final syllable. Therefore, Americans abroad are *travelers*, while peripatetic Brits are *travellers.*

Another wrinkle involves words where the vowel-consonant pattern would normally indicate a long vowel, but the pronunciation is short, as in *head* or *come.* In this case, if we add a suffix, there is no need to protect the short vowel by doubling the consonant: *heading* rhymes with *wedding*, not with *reading*, while *coming* rhymes with *humming*, not with *homing.*

There are of course anomalies and exceptions, but following these guidelines will help you minimize your errors

Practice 18

The following paragraph contains several of the spelling errors described in this section. Locate and correct the commonly misspelled words. There are 37 spelling errors in the paragraph in all. Answers are found on page 83.

Many people think it is alright to except charitable assistance irregardless of their ability to secure financial independance for themselves. Other people think it can not effect them, or that they do not loose money, if these proffesional charity cases force the government to acomodate they're free reign. I would not be exxagerating if I said that noone lives in a vaccum, and all descent people need to be responsable for there own welfare to. I wander if it would of ever ocured too these folks to ascent to by food, clothing, and shelter firsthand for people who will not altar their indiscrete financial habits. I think its unlikely. When your looking passed the question of whose paying for these goods and services, than your excepting there right to steel from you're pocket everyday.

Practice 19

Find and mark up the mistake(s) in the following sentences. Answers are found on page 83 .

1. In fields such as human developement and family planing, it is becomming easier to find funding for basic research.

2. As the hailstorm intensified, the campers paniced and ran screamming through the grounds.

3. Effective leadership means recognizing when an objective cannot be reached without sacrificing essential resources.

Homonyms and Other Commonly Confused Words

Accept or *except*? *Alter* or *altar*? *Discrete* or *discreet*? Even if you know the difference between these words, when you're under time pressure, it's easy to type in the wrong one. Homonyms and contractions (e.g., *who's*) are especially good candidates for typos, so here's a quick review of some of the most common troublemakers.

Note: Since we reviewed contractions vs. possessives already, they aren't included in the list below. Remember that you can avoid contraction typos by simply avoiding contractions throughout your essay. (Besides, many professors feel strongly that contractions are not appropriate in academic prose.)

accept (v.): to take or receive. *The CEO <u>accepted</u> the treasurer's resignation.*
except (prep.): leave out. *The Town Council approved all elements of the proposal <u>except</u> the tax increase.*

adverse (adj.): unfavorable. *This plan would have an <u>adverse</u> impact on the environment.*
averse (adj.): opposed or reluctant. *I am <u>averse</u> to doing business with companies that don't treat their employees fairly.*

advice (n.): recommendation as to what should be done. *I would like your <u>advice</u> about how to handle this situation.*
advise (v.): to recommend what should be done. *I will be happy to <u>advise</u> you.*

affect (v.): to have an impact or influence on. The expansion of Pyramid Shopping Mall will certainly <u>affect</u> traffic on the access roads.
effect (n.): result, impact. *The proposal will have a deleterious <u>effect</u> on everyone's quality of life.* (v.): to cause, implement. *The engineers were able to <u>effect</u> a change in train's performance at high speeds.*

altar (n.): an elevated structure, typically intended for the performance of religious rituals. *The court refused to allow the construction of an <u>altar</u> on public property.*
alter (v.): to change. *It should be a simple matter to <u>alter</u> one's will.*

among (prep): used to compare three or more items or entities. *We can choose from <u>among</u> dozens of styles.*
between (prep): used to compare two items or entities. *We can choose <u>between</u> these two styles.*

amoral (adj.): neither moral nor immoral; without a sense of moral judgment. *Claire was upset with the <u>amoral</u> discussion of terrorist acts.*
immoral (adj.): morally wrong. *Whatever beliefs a terrorist has, terrorist acts are <u>immoral</u>.*

ascent (n.): climb, upward movement. *Vanessa's rapid <u>ascent</u> up the corporate ladder impressed us all.*
assent (n.): agreement; (v.): to agree. *Peter has given his <u>assent</u> to the plan.*

assure (v.): to convince or guarantee. *He has <u>assured</u> me that this is a safe investment.*

ensure (v.): to make certain. *Please <u>ensure</u> that this is a safe investment.*

insure (v.): to guard against loss. *There is no way to <u>insure</u> this investment.*

bazaar (n.): traditional oriental market. *I found these fantastic trinkets at the <u>bazaar</u>.*

bizarre (adj.): very strange, weird. *No one knew how to respond to such a <u>bizarre</u> question.*

cite (v.): to quote, to refer. *The article <u>cited</u> our annual report.*

sight (n.): something seen or visible; the faculty of seeing. *What an amazing <u>sight</u>!*

site (n.): location; (v.): to place or locate. *This is the perfect <u>site</u> for a new office.*

complement (n.): something that completes; (v.): to go with or complete. *This item really <u>complements</u> our product line.*

compliment (v.): to flatter; (n.): a flattering remark. *That was a <u>sincere</u> compliment.*

continual (adj.): repeated regularly and frequently. *Alan's <u>continual</u> telephone calls finally wore Rosa down and she agreed to a meeting.*

continuous (adj.): extended or prolonged without interruption. *The <u>continuous</u> banging from the construction site gave me a severe headache.*

decent (adj.): proper, acceptable. *You can trust Lena to do what is <u>decent</u>.*

descent (n.): downward movement. *The rapid <u>descent</u> of the balloon frightened its riders.*

discrete (adj.): separate, not connected. *These are two <u>discrete</u> issues.*

discreet (adj.): prudent, modest, having discretion; not allowing others to notice. *I must be very <u>discreet</u> about looking for a new job while I am still employed here.*

disinterested (adj.): impartial, objective. *We need a <u>disinterested</u> person to act as an arbitrator in this dispute.*

uninterested (adj.): not interested. *Charles is <u>uninterested</u>, but he'll come along anyway.*

eminent (adj.): outstanding, distinguished. *The <u>eminent</u> Judge Blackwell will teach a special seminar in business ethics this fall.*

imminent (adj.): about to happen, impending. *Warned of <u>imminent</u> layoffs, Loretta began looking for another job.*

incidence (uncountable noun: occurrence) frequency

incident *(pl.: incidents)* (countable noun: events, cases)

personal (adj.): private or pertaining to the individual. *Please mark the envelope "<u>personal</u> and confidential."*

personnel (n.): employees. *This year we had a 5% increase in <u>personnel</u>.*

precede (v.): to come before. *The list of resources should <u>precede</u> the financial worksheet.*

proceed (v.): to go forward. *Although Jules will be absent, we will <u>proceed</u> with the meeting as planned.*

principal (n.) head of a school or organization, primary participant, main sum of money; (adj.): main, foremost, most important. *Joshua is one of the <u>principals</u> of the company.*

principle (n.): a basic truth or law. *I have always run my business based on the <u>principle</u> that honesty is the best policy, even in a capitalist society.*

rein (n.) a means of restraint or guidance; (v.) to restrain, control. *You need to <u>rein</u> in your intern, Carol—she's taking on much too much responsibility and doesn't seem to know what she's doing.*

reign (v.) to exercise power; (n.): period in which a ruler exercised power or a condition prevailed. *Under the <u>reign</u> of King Richard, order was restored.*

than (conj.): used to compare. *I will be more successful this time because I am more experienced <u>than</u> before.*

then (adv.): at that time, therefore. *I was very naïve back <u>then</u>.*

weather (n.): climatic conditions, state of the atmosphere. *The bad <u>weather</u> is going to keep people away from our grand opening.*

whether (conj.): used to refer to a choice between alternatives. *I am not sure <u>whether</u> I will attend the grand opening or not.*

Practice 20

Find and mark up the mistake(s) in the following sentences. Answers are found on page 83.

1. Its often necessary to by more goods then can be consumed in a single day even though there likely to spoil.

2. I would of thought that journalists should avoid taking sides when they right about such controversial subjects.

3. We all here stories of people who's children refuse to accompany them on vacations.

4. Can you site three incidences in the passed in which Congress has given its ascent to such a proposal?

5. The board of education excepted the advise of the high school principle in chosing to altar the wording of the teachers' contracts.

6. After years of suffering under the heal of an autocrat, the citizens must steal themselves for change.

MAXIM 2: BE CLEAR

Correctness is important, but it means little if your sentences are not clear. Ambiguous, vague, and just plain confusing sentences can result from poor sentence structure or ineffective word choice. Since you have a limited amount of space for the LSAT Writing Sample (the equivalent of two sheets of paper), it is imperative that your sentences and word choices are as precise as possible.

Use Straightforward Sentence Structure

Some writers strive to impress readers by writing elaborate sentences—but those sentences can often get tangled. Don't force your reader to untangle your ideas! Doing so will lessen the efficacy of your argument. Seek clarity and stick to straightforward sentence structure: *subject, verb, indirect object, object*.

That doesn't mean you can't write sophisticated sentences with lots of phrases and clauses. But you will need to be especially careful about where you put modifying clauses and phrases. The basic rule: Make sure your modifiers are as close as possible to the words they modify.

Modifier Placement

In English, the position of the word within a sentence often establishes the word's relationship to other words in the sentence. This is especially true with modifying phrases. Like pronouns, adjectival expressions are generally connected to the nearest word that agrees with the modifier in person and number. Likewise, when a sentence contains more than one verb or verbal element (such as an infinitive, gerund, or participial), an adverbial expression will be interpreted as modifying the closest verb. The placement of prepositional phrases is particularly important, since they can modify both nouns and verbs as well as other elements.

> AMBIGUOUS: The president and his closest advisors frequently discuss potential scandals behind closed doors
>
> > [*Which generally occur* behind closed doors—*the* discussions *or the* scandals?]
>
> CLEAR: Behind closed doors, the president and his closest advisors frequently discuss potential scandals.
>
> CLEAR: The president and his closest advisors frequently discuss potential scandals that are occurring behind closed doors.
>
> AMBIGUOUS: A politician must consider what compensation is expected for each campaign donation at the time it is given.
>
> > [*Does* at the time it is given *modify* consider *or* expected?]
>
> CLEAR: When accepting a campaign donation, a politician must consider what compensation is expected.
>
> CLEAR: When a politician receives a campaign donation, he or she must consider what compensation a donor expects in return.

Many adverbial expressions can refer to words that either precede or follow them. Ambiguity can result when the modifier is squeezed between two possible referents and the reader has no way to know which is the intended referent:

AMBIGUOUS: The pharmaceutical company announced <u>suddenly</u> researchers had succeeded in identifying the neurotoxin.

[*Which was sudden—the company's announcement or the researchers' success?*]

CLEAR: <u>Suddenly</u>, the pharmaceutical company announced that researchers had succeeded in identifying the neurotoxin.

CLEAR: The pharmaceutical company announced that researchers had <u>suddenly</u> succeeded in identifying the neurotoxin.

[*Notice how the use of* that *before the noun clause makes the sentence easier to understand.*]

Avoid Vague or Ambiguous Language

Vague words are unclear; ambiguous words are words that have more than one possible meaning.

Vague Words and Phrases

Words like *lots, somewhat,* and *really* are vague. How much exactly? Your sentences will be clearer and more powerful if you use words that are more precise:

VAGUE: We saw <u>lots of</u> improvement in employee morale over the last six months.

MORE EXACT: We saw <u>significant</u> improvement in employee morale over the last six months.

VAGUE: Our choices for subcontractors are <u>somewhat</u> limited.

MORE EXACT: Our choices for subcontractors are <u>severely</u> limited.

Unclear and Ambiguous Pronoun References

A pronoun is a word that stands in for a noun (or noun expression) in a sentence. A pronoun must agree with its antecedent and must refer clearly to one and only one antecedent.

AMBIGUOUS: No entrepreneur should tell a client that he is overly concerned with image.

[*Does* he *refer to* entrepreneur *or* client?]

CLEAR: No entrepreneur should accuse a client of being overly concerned with image.

CLEAR: Being overly concerned with image is not something that an entrepreneur should admit to a client. *or* No entrepreneur should admit being overly concerned with image to a client.

Occasionally, you may have to repeat a noun, rather than rely on a pronoun that may make your sentence ambiguous.

AMBIGUOUS: It may be cost effective to rely on subcontractors instead of company personnel, as they would certainly require extra training.

[*Who would require training—the* subcontractors *or the* company personnel?]

CLEAR: It may be cost effective to rely on subcontractors instead of company personnel, as the company personnel would certainly require extra training.

An antecedent must actually occur in your text. Even if you think the reader will know what you mean, do not use a pronoun without a clear and appropriate antecedent.

> INCORRECT: When you are voting for a candidate, you must be sure he or she is fully qualified to undertake it.

> > [*What does* it *refer to? The antecedent is implied but must be clearly stated.*]

> CORRECT: When you are voting, you must be sure the candidate you choose is fully qualified to undertake the position in question.

Avoid using *this, that, it,* or *which* to refer to a whole phrase, sentence, or idea. Even when these pronouns are placed very close to their intended antecedents, the references may still be unclear.

> UNCLEAR: U.S. consumers use increasingly large amounts of nonrecyclable diapers every year. Some worry that this will someday turn the Earth into a giant trash can.

> > [*What exactly is* this? *The use of diapers or the trash that results from their use?*]

> CLEAR: U.S. consumers use increasingly large amounts of non-recyclable diapers every year. Some worry that this ever-growing mass of waste products will someday turn the Earth into a giant trash can.

> UNCLEAR: The candidate changed his position on all the key issues, which made the voters extremely nervous.

> > [What makes the voters nervous—that the candidate changed position or the issues? *Which* could refer to either.]

> CLEAR: The candidate changed his position on all the key issues, making the voters extremely nervous.

Ambiguous repetition generally involves pronouns or other words which may refer to multiple entities or concepts:

> UNACCEPTABLE: <u>They</u> concluded that most teachers do like <u>their</u> students, and, while <u>they</u> may not clearly express <u>their</u> feelings, <u>they</u> generally do reciprocate <u>this</u> sympathy.

> ACCEPTABLE: The <u>researchers</u> concluded that most teachers do like their students, and, while the <u>children</u> may not clearly express their feelings, they generally reciprocate their <u>teacher's</u> sympathy.

> UNACCEPTABLE: It is well known <u>that that</u> problem has been the subject of a full-fledged investigation, and <u>that</u> will most likely yield some temporary solution <u>that</u> will prove acceptable to all concerned parties.

> ACCEPTABLE: It is well known that the problem has been the subject of a full-fledged investigation, which will most likely yield a temporary solution acceptable to all concerned parties.

MAXIM 3: BE CONCISE

Why take 200 words to express an idea that can be conveyed in 100? Unfortunately, some of us have been "trained" to use more words than necessary because we were often under pressure to write essays of a certain length. But 100 clear and concise words are much better than 200 words of fluff.

And the way to move from 100 to 200 words if so required isn't through "filler" words and phrases—it's through the development of ideas. Unnecessary words and phrases don't improve writing; they bog it down and often irritate readers. Concise writing is clear writing; it avoids the clutter and confusion that often result from unnecessary wordiness.

This is especially important to remember as you prepare for your LSAT Writing Sample. You will only have 35 minutes to make your argument. If you start adding fluff words you may run out of time before you have made a credible case for your position. And since you have a limited amount of space on the Writing Sample Response Sheet, you may run out of space, too!

Wordy Phrases

In an attempt to make their prose seem more scholarly or more formal, some test takers use phrases where single words will do: *at the present time* or *at this point in time* instead of *now,* or *take into consideration* instead of simply *consider.* Don't. Instead, use the simpler, clearer phrase. Here are some more examples of wordy phrases and their concise counterparts:

along the lines of	*like*
as a matter of fact	*in fact*
at all times	*always*
by means of	*by*
because of the fact that	*because*
by virtue of the fact that	*because*
due to the fact that	*because*
for the reason that	*because*
in light of the fact that	*because*
in this day and age	*today*
in order to	*to*
in spite of the fact that	*although, though*
in the event that	*if*
until such a time as	*until*

Unnecessary Relative Clauses

Wordiness is also caused by unnecessary *that, who,* and *which* clauses and phrases. To be more concise and precise, remove the relative pronoun and verb to create an appositive or turn the phrases and clauses into adjectives:

WORDY: The Truman Doctrine, which was established in 1947, created a "policy of containment."

CONCISE: Established in 1947, the Truman Doctrine created a "policy of containment."

MORE CONCISE: The 1947 Truman Doctrine created a "policy of containment."

WORDY: Temporary employees who work hard and are loyal are often rewarded with full-time employment.

CONCISE: Hard-working, loyal temporary employees are often rewarded with full-time employment

Cluttered Constructions

There is, it is, and *that* often unnecessarily clutter sentences. A simple deletion or reconstruction can eliminate wordiness and create smoother sentences.

WORDY: It is essential that all visitors and employees wear safety goggles on the production floor.

CONCISE: All visitors and employees must wear safety goggles on the production floor.

WORDY: There is another reason that we should switch vendors, and that is that our current vendor does not offer bulk discounts.

CONCISE: We should also switch vendors because our current supplier does not offer bulk discounts.

Unnecessary Repetition

It is redundant to speak of "a beginner lacking experience": the word *beginner* in itself implies lack of experience. Yet we sometimes use repetitive phrases, especially when we are unsure that we are expressing our idea clearly or with sufficient force.

REDUNDANT	CONCISE
refer back	*refer*
few in number	*few*
small-sized	*small*
grouped together	*grouped*
in my own personal opinion	*in my opinion*
end result	*result*
serious crisis	*crisis*
new initiatives	*initiatives*
climb up	*climb*

Sometime a sentence unnecessarily "defines" a word again in an attempt to make an idea more clear:

WORDY: Jared lost a lot of business because of inflation, which drove up prices. [Inflation *means an increase in prices, so the clause* which drove up prices *is entirely unnecessary.*]

CONCISE: Jared lost a lot of business because of inflation.

WORDY: He is sad and depressed because he did not get promoted to a better position.

    [Sad *and* depressed *are synonyms;* promoted *means to move up to a better position.*]

CONCISE: He is depressed because he did not get the promotion.

MAXIM 4: BE EXACT

The more precise your language, the more impact your words will have. You can avoid wordiness and add power to your writing by using exact words and phrases.

    IMPRECISE: Paris is a <u>very beautiful</u> city.

    PRECISE: Paris is a <u>stunning</u> city.

Stunning is more precise, more concise, and more sophisticated than *very beautiful*—and thus a better word choice.

    IMPRECISE: After a while, the odor disappeared into the air.

    PRECISE: After a while, the odor dissipated.

    IMPRECISE: The school had to close because it had many problems with safety.

    PRECISE: The school was shut down because of many safety violations. [Violations *is more specific and concrete than* problems with; shut down *is more exact and powerful than* had to close.

MAXIM 5: BE APPROPRIATE

Being appropriate means writing at the appropriate level of formality. You need a style, tone, and point of view that show respect for your readers—their authority, their level of intelligence, and their time. For the LSAT Writing Sample, this means presenting your argument with a fairly high level of formality. In your personal statement, however, you can inject a little more of your personality. In fact, the goal of the personal statement is to show admissions officers who you are. So, while your personal statement should still be written in a formal style, it should not be so formal that is reads as stiff or like an academic essay.

Avoid Slang and Colloquial Expressions

There are many levels of diction, and each genre has a range of dictions generally considered appropriate. Your essays do not require the most formal diction, but an overly colloquial style is not appropriate, and slang of any kind should be strictly avoided. Colloquial language isn't exactly slang, but it is informal and for the most part should also be avoided. Here are some particular expressions to avoid, as well as some acceptable substitutes.

Intensifiers

Awfully, incredibly, pretty, really, totally: all these words have legitimate uses, but they should not be used as generic intensifiers. Even *very* has been so overused that it tends to diminish rather than emphasize your point. Preferable alternatives include:

absolutely	*indispensably*
acutely	*notably*
amply	*particularly*
astonishingly	*positively*
authentically	*powerfully*
certainly	*prodigiously*
considerably	*profoundly*
decidedly	*remarkably*
deeply	*substantially*
eminently	*superlatively*
emphatically	*surpassingly*
exceedingly	*surprisingly*
excessively	*terribly*
extensively	*truly*
extraordinarily	*uncommonly*
extremely	*unusually*
genuinely	*vastly*
greatly	*way*
highly	*wonderfully*

Down-toners

Kind of, sort of, pretty much—again, these expressions have legitimate uses, but not in a formal essay. Besides being too colloquial, these terms are also vague. Instead use words such as *fairly, partially, largely, mildly, moderately, quite, rather, slightly, somewhat.*

Quantifiers

Instead of *lots, a lot of, a bunch of,* and other colloquial (and vague) quantifiers, try *many, much, a number of, a substantial number of, quite a few, numerous.*

Contractions

Coulda, gonna, hafta, hadta, lotsa, oughta, shoulda, wanna, woulda: we use these all the time in speech, but these colloquial contractions are not acceptable in formal writing.

Use Sophisticated Vocabulary

An appropriate style for the LSAT Writing Sample requires a formal and refined level of vocabulary. Here are a few simple substitutes to help you write on a more sophisticated level.

- Instead of *like*, use *such as:*

  DEPRECATED: The success of a business depends on many factors, <u>like</u> convenient location, well-trained staff, and effective promotion.

  ACCEPTABLE: The success of a business depends on many factors, <u>such as</u> convenient location, well-trained staff, and effective promotion.

- Instead of *different*, use *various.*

- Instead of *big*, use *large, important, substantial, prestigious, significant.*

- Instead of *okay*, use *acceptable, satisfactory, appropriate.*

- Instead of *etc.,* use *and so on* (better yet, restructure the list and use *including* or *for example* or *include more examples*).

- Instead of *oftentimes*, use *often.*

  UNSOPHISTICATED: For <u>different</u> reasons, I was <u>turned down</u> by <u>a lot</u> of <u>big</u> schools, <u>like</u> Harvard, Yale, Princeton, Dartmouth, <u>etc</u>.

  SOPHISTICATED: For <u>various</u> reasons, I was <u>rejected</u> by <u>many</u> <u>prestigious</u> schools, including Harvard, Yale, Princeton, and Dartmouth.

Avoid Jargon and Pretentious Language

Sophisticated does not mean *pretentious*. Pretentious texts try to impress by sounding scholarly or profound, often using over-the-top or esoteric vocabulary. You can be sophisticated without clouding meaning or annoying readers with pretentious language.

　　PRETENTIOUS: Avoid periphrasis and pleonasms in your compositions.

　　JUST RIGHT: Avoid wordiness and redundancy in your writing.

Jargon is technical or specialized language. Remember the rule: respect your reader. Some of the admissions officers who read your essays will be familiar with specialized terms but there may be a few who will be confused by your word choice. So, either avoid jargon altogether and use lay terms or define any specialized language you use.

Practice 21

Find and mark up the mistake(s) in the following sentences. Answers are found on page 83.

1. Lots of people are incredibly into video games and watching the tube, and I basically feel that that's okay, although it's pretty much of a waste of time.

2. These days there're a lot of different reality shows, like *Survivor, American Idol,* etc., that are all kind of similar.

3. Oftentimes a perfectly good plan can be trashed by a minor oversight.

Practice 22

The following paragraph contains several examples of slang and substandard vocabulary. Rewrite the paragraph in a style more appropriate for the LSAT. Answers are found on page 83.

It is really pretty supportable to argue that studying an academic discipline changes your view of the world. Like say if you study history, you oftentimes read about a bunch of different facts that are equally as important as the ones you learned about in school, but that totally weren't covered. Lots of big social trends and beliefs that we think shoulda been okay at this point in time turn out to be incredibly bogus. Studying a discipline like history can really change how we look at the world.

_____

_____

_____

_____

_____

_____

_____

_____

_____

_____

_____

_____

_____

_____

_____

Use an Appropriate Point of View

Though some professors still preach "Don't use *I*," especially in your personal statement, your readers are expecting you to express your opinion. So use the first person point of view, but not excessively—you don't need *I* in every sentence. Just write assertively (see Maxim 7). Use your personal experiences as examples throughout, but don't overdo it. You can also address your readers as *you* (second person point of view), but don't address them directly (e.g., *dear reader*), and don't attribute words, ideas, or experiences to your readers. Your reader *may not* have seen or might not believe or might not know. Play it safe by using the generic third person (but not *one*, which often comes off sounding pretentious):.

> WRONG: As you know . . .
>
> WRONG: As one knows . . .
>
> RIGHT: As many people know . . .
>
> WRONG: You have undoubtedly seen . . .
>
> RIGHT: As you may have seen . . .

MAXIM 6: BE CONSISTENT

While variety is important in some aspects of writing (see Maxim 8), **consistency** is an important element your readers will be looking for in your LSAT Writing Sample. Consistency in writing shows evidence of control over your thoughts as well as the conventions of writing. Make sure your essay is consistent in style and tone as well as point of view.

Consistent Style

Style is created primarily through word choice and sentence structure. Do you tend to write in long, descriptive sentences? In a short, bare-bones kind of style? Do you prefer words like *perambulate* and *hirsute* to *walk around* and *hairy*? You know that the most appropriate style for your essays is formal but not stiff or pretentious (see Maxim 5). If you tend to write in a very informal style, fancy up a bit when you write your personal statement and prepare for the LSAT Writing Sample. Don't try to sound like someone else—stick to your natural voice—but choose words and sentence structures that are more sophisticated than normal. Whatever your natural style, start with an appropriate style and stick to it throughout your essay. A shift in style suggests an inconsistent grasp of the material, a lack of confidence in your own writing skills, or a gap in logic—all of which can be quite disconcerting to your readers.

> INCONSISTENT: Lots of things can work together to create success, including education, smarts, foresight, perseverance, and sometimes plain old dumb luck.
>
> CONSISTENT: Many factors contribute to success, including education, intelligence, foresight, perseverance, and sometimes serendipity.
>
> INCONSISTENT: The reef is a vast ecosystem in the sea where a bunch of species live together. Lots of them are mutually dependent upon each other.
>
> CONSISTENT: The reef is a vast ecosystem in the sea where hundreds of species live in symbiotic relationships.

Consistent Tone

Tone is the mood or attitude conveyed by writing or speech. In text, we convey tone through word choice, sentence structure, and punctuation. For example, both of the sentences below say the same thing, but the word choice and punctuation convey a different attitude towards the senator's action.

> The senator <u>evaded</u> another question.

> The senator <u>dodged</u> another question!

You might have a great sense of humor, but your Writing Sample is not the place for a light-hearted or jocular essay. The most appropriate tone is one that is serious, informative, and always respectful of readers and other points of view. Start with an appropriate tone and stick to it throughout the essay.

Consistent Point of View

It is often useful to explore contrasting points of view within your essay—in fact, consideration of other opinions is one of the hallmarks of an effective argument. But your point of view as *author* should remain consistent within your essay. It is easy, for example, to slide around from *I* to *you* to *one* to *we.* The effect can be disconcerting, to say the least. One option to avoid is the use of *one*: it is grammatically limiting and it sounds pretentious. Whatever narrative voice you choose, and whichever voices you introduce to represent other perspectives, be consistent (but avoid overuse of particular pronouns).

> TANGLED: I often feel that one has to make sacrifices to reach the goals you set for yourself, but we should always remember that life occurs in the present tense.

> STRAIGHTFORWARD: I often feel that I must make sacrifices to reach my goal, but I try to remember that life occurs in the present tense.

> STRAIGHTFORWARD: We may feel it necessary to make sacrifices in order to reach our goals, but we should always remember that life occurs in the present tense.

> STRAIGHTFORWARD: Some people feel it necessary to make sacrifices in order to reach their goals, but they should always remember that life occurs in the present tense.

> STRAIGHTFORWARD: You may feel it necessary to make sacrifices in order to reach your goals, but you should always remember that life occurs in the present tense.

MAXIM 7: BE ASSERTIVE

An assertive essay expresses confidence in its ideas, and this makes the essay far more convincing than one that is hesitant. Remember that the LSAT Writing Sample is an argument in support of one of the choices provided in the scenario—so **state your points without hesitation**.

> HESITANT: In my humble opinion, there are few things more important to leading a company through a relatively successful expansion than having a plan that includes, among other things, communication and customer service.

> ASSERTIVE: Communication and customer service are essential components of an expansion plan.

HESITANT: I think maybe we could come up with some way to make chief executives more accountable for what they do.

ASSERTIVE: Chief executives should be more accountable for their actions.

The more assertive sentences convey confidence, which goes a long way towards convincing readers of a particular point of view. They are also clearer and more concise than the hesitant versions.

On the other hand, there is no need to bludgeon the graders with your certitude. Remember that an effective argument includes consideration of the other point of view. A few qualifiers will give the impression that you are reasonable: *fairly, rather, somewhat, relatively,* and of such expressions as *seems to be, a little,* and *a certain amount of* are good choices. But do not overplay the modesty card.

TOO ASSERTIVE: In light of the facts, it is absolutely certain that the election scandal could have been avoided.

TOO MODEST: In light of the facts, it seems fairly reasonable that perhaps the election scandal might have been avoided. [Too wordy as well.]

JUST RIGHT: In light of the facts, it seems certain that the election scandal could have been avoided.

Avoid Needless Self-Reference

While you will present your point of view in your LSAT Writing Sample, it is unnecessary to label every assertion as opinion. One or two self-references *may* be appropriate, but there is no need to draw attention to yourself. Keep your focus on the topic.

OVERLY SELF-REFERENT: I used to believe that we should have a choice on matters of personal safety such as whether or not to wear a helmet when riding a motorcycle, but I now realize that personal safety is actually a matter of public welfare.

JUST RIGHT: Personal safety is a matter of public welfare.

BEST FOR AN OPENING PARAGRAPH: I believe personal safety is a matter of public welfare.

Use the Active Voice

Let's be clear: the passive voice is an extremely useful device, particularly for expressing ideas where the speaker does not know the agent or does not wish to reveal it:

EXAMPLE: Recently, two schools in my district were vandalized.

The passive is also useful in manipulating sentence balance, particularly when the subject is long and involved and the predicate is brief.

AWKWARD: Often, newspapers that are having problems with falling circulation, rising costs, and the threat of a hostile buy-out from an international publishing conglomerate hire media consultants.

BETTER: Often, media consultants are hired by newspapers that are having problems with falling circulation, rising costs, and the threat of a hostile buy-out from an international publishing conglomerate.

However . . .the passive has been notoriously overused by weak writers trying to sound authoritative, to the point that readers generally react negatively to it. Solution: **wherever possible, use the active voice**. Active sentences are more direct and more concise, conveying your ideas with more clarity and power.

>PASSIVE: The active voice should be used by essay writers.

>ACTIVE: Essay writers should use the active voice.

Practice 23

The following sentences use passive voice unnecessarily. Rewrite them in active voice. Answers are found on page 83.

1. The coolant pumps were destroyed by a surge of power.

   _____

   _____

2. The transformer was struck by a bolt of lightning.

   _____

   _____

3. The goalkeeper was too slow to stop the ball.

   _____

   _____

4. The moods of a manic-depressive are unpredictable.

   _____

   _____

5. The administrative secretary is responsible for monitoring and balancing the budgets.

   _____

   _____

6. It is important that hikers remain on marked trails.

   _____

   _____

7. All too often, athletes with marginal academic skills have been recruited by our coaches.

   _____

   _____

8. Teachers have been portrayed or stereotyped by the media as illiterate, even though they fulfill strict requirements.

   _____

   _____

MAXIM 8: BE EXCITING

Whatever you actually *say* in your essay, *how* you say it can have a significant impact on how impressed admissions officers are with your writing. Your essay can be correct, concise, appropriate—all of the other maxims—yet still be dull and dry and at risk for hurting your overall application. This is particularly the case with your personal statement. If your essay is boring, your readers may think the same is true of you. You can make your Writing Sample and your personal statement inviting to readers by having variety in both your sentence structure and vocabulary.

Variety in Sentence Structure

The best essays contain a variety of sentence forms. What that means, specifically, is that you'll want to use a combination of simple, compound, complex, and compound-complex sentences. Here are some examples:

Simple (one main clause): Any entrepreneur seeking a new business location should seriously consider Nashville, Tennessee.

Compound (two or more main clauses): Entrepreneurs often need to select a new business location, and they should seriously consider Nashville, Tennessee.

Complex (one main clause, one subordinate clause): If any entrepreneurs are looking for a new business location, they should seriously consider Nashville Tennessee.

Compound-complex (two or more main clauses, plus at least one subordinate clause): Entrepreneurs often need to select a new business location, and when they do, they should seriously consider Nashville, Tennessee.

Practice 24

Fill in the table below. Each sentence is provided in either simple, compound, complex, or compound-complex form. Fill in the table by rewriting each given example in the three other forms. Answers are found on page 84.

Simple	Sometimes the fresh perspective of a nonexpert can be valuable in the consideration of a subject.
Compound	
Complex	
Compound-Complex	

Simple	
Compound	The feeling of having fulfilled a personal goal is important, but the tangible rewards of society are at least as important.
Complex	
Compound-Complex	

Simple	
Compound	
Complex	Even though Company B is more expensive, the important question is whether the combined cost of pest control and savings in product damage are greater with Company B.
Compound-Complex	

Simple	
Compound	
Complex	
Compound-Complex	Different academic communities have different traditions, and while these differences may be significant, it is an oversimplification to say that there can be no meaningful interaction between them.

Simple	It is reasonable to argue that a cheaper brand of sunscreen might encourage people to have a false sense of security.
Compound	
Complex	
Compound-Complex	

In addition to using a variety of these basic sentence forms, you can enliven your sentences by placing "interrupters," phrases, and clauses in various places:

X is unlike Y because of Z.

Because of Z, X is unlike Y.

However, X is unlike Y because of Z.

X, however, is unlike Y because of Z.

However, because of Z, X is unlike Y.

Length

Varying sentence length throughout creates a more pleasing rhythm for your readers—too many short sentences are likely to sound monotonous while too many long sentences may be difficult on your reader. A short sentence (four to eight words) can effectively emphasize a simple point; a long sentence (30–45 words) might be necessary to present a relatively complicated idea.

EXAMPLE: Entrepreneurs often need to select a new business location, and when they do, they should seriously consider Nashville, Tennessee. This southern city has a great deal to offer.

Sentence Openers

How you *start* your sentences should vary, too. If all of your sentences start with the subject, even if the sentence lengths and forms vary, it can sound awfully monotonous (*unless* you are purposely using parallel construction).

MONOTONOUS: Nashville was founded in 1779. Tenessee became the sixteenth state of the union in 1796. Nashville became the state's capitol in 1812.

EXCITING: Founded in 1779, Nashville became the capitol of Tennessee in 1812, sixteen years after Tennessee became the sixteenth state of the union.

To add variety, combine sentences as in the example above and start some sentences with introductory clauses and phrases rather than the subject. But keep the basic order for sentence structure for your core clause (subject, verb, indirect object, object).

NEEDS VARIETY: Nashville was founded in 1779. It became the state capitol in 1812.

HAS VARIETY: Founded in 1779, Nashville became the state capitol in 1812.

A Varied Vocabulary

Repetition is one of our most effective rhetorical devices. When used ineffectively or thoughtlessly, repetition can seem excessive and make your reader think that you have a limited vocabulary. Strive to show your diversity of vocabulary by using synonyms instead of relying on a few key words throughout your essay.

REPETITIVE VOCABULARY: <u>Business</u> is not an occupation for the faint of heart. Every <u>businessperson</u> should be aware that nearly 50 percent of <u>businesses</u> fail in their first year, while 75 percent of <u>businesses</u> go under within three years. Our first order of <u>business</u> in this essay is to consider the question, "What are the causes of <u>business</u> failure?"

SYNONYM-ENRICHED: <u>Business</u> is not an occupation for the faint of heart. Every <u>entrepreneur</u> should be aware that nearly 50 percent of new <u>ventures</u> fail in their first year, while 75 percent go under within three years. Our first <u>concern</u> in this essay is to consider the question, "What are the causes of <u>commercial</u> failure?"

An effective way to avoid repetition is to make lists of terms pertinent to recent Writing Sample topics (see page 5 in Chapter 1 for a list of recent topics). For example, here is a clustered list of nouns that might be useful in preparing an argument when the scenario relates to higher education.

- facilities, campus, library, dormitory, laboratory, location, faculty-to-student ratio, sports

- recruitment, scholarship, financial aid, stipend, assistance, promotional material, catalogue, publication, publicity, public relations

- admissions, requirements, standards, entrance, application

- administration, administrator, dean, official, board of trustees, committee

- faculty, professor, advisor, candidate, academic, researcher, lecturer, teaching assistant, educator

- student, applicant, candidate, alumnus, registrant, freshman, sophomore, junior, senior, undergraduate, graduate, scholar, researcher

- field, major, research, study, discipline, program

- instruction, courses, curriculum, elective, required course, lecture, seminar, workshop, lab, syllabus, assigned readings, assignments, homework

- grades, marks, scores, average, points, GPA

- test, competition, examination, quiz, midterm, final

- college, university, institution, higher education, academia, school, junior college,

- goals, objectives, degree, graduation, commencement, employment, career, job, placement, opportunity

Practice 25

The following paragraph contains examples of overly repetitive word use. Correct the problems by rewriting the paragraph with appropriate synonyms in place of the repetitive words and phrases. Answers are found on page 85.

Courses that focus on intellectual development are more important than courses that contribute to professional development. Courses focused on professional development assume that these courses will still be relevant to the future job market, while in fact the constant changes in the job market might make such courses obsolete. In contrast, courses that work toward intellectual development are courses that train a person for a variety of job market roles, so that even if the job market changes, the work done in the courses remains relevant. This is not to say that many courses cannot do both: preparing a person for the job market while also preparing her for a variety of different job market possibilities. But, while courses on professional development have their place in the realm of university courses, they should not be allowed to supersede courses that train the intellect for a changing job market.

_____

_____

_____

_____

_____

_____

_____

_____

_____

_____

_____

_____

_____

_____

_____

_____

_____

_____

_____

_____

_____

EIGHT MAXIMS, REDUX

Here's a quick recap of our eight maxims of effective writing:

1. Be correct.
2. Be clear.
3. Be concise.
4. Be exact.
5. Be appropriate.
6. Be consistent.
7. Be assertive.
8. Be exciting.

Check your answers to the practice exercises from this chapter on the following page. Let's take what you have learned about grammar, mechanics, and style and apply it to the Writing Sample in the next chapter. Chapter 3 will cover how to write essays on test day.

ANSWERS AND EXPLANATIONS

Practice 1

1. Most of us wish that our parents <u>were</u> better prepared to face retirement.

2. While we may wish that our physical conditioning <u>were</u> better, few of us are prepared to invest the time and effort in the kind of exercise and diet that might help us achieve it.

3. No mistake.

4. No mistake.

5. No mistake.

6. Judging from recent pricing patterns, it is imperative that the American government <u>begin</u> to regulate retail milk prices

Practice 2

1. **Many** people in New York **travel** by subway.
   Many is a singular indefinite pronoun.

2. **Workers** in New York often **commute** a long way to work.
   The prepositional phrase *in New York* interferes with the connection between the plural subject, *workers* and the plural verb *commute*.

3. **Tourists** in New York **expect** to see the subway.
   The prepositional phrase *in New York* separates the plural subject *tourists* and the plural verb *expect*.

4. The "redbird" subway **cars** with a red body **have** been a common sight in New York until recently.
   The prepositional phrase *with a red body* might mislead you about the connection between the plural subject *cars* and the plural verb *have been*.

5. The **streets** of large cities such as New York **are** undercut by complex networks of subway tunnels.
   The long-distance phrases *of large cities such as New York* interferes with your perception of the relationship between the plural subject *streets* and the plural verb *are*.

6. Today, the **economy** of New York and other large cities **is** booming.
   The word *cities* next to the verb can interfere with your sense that the subject *economy* matches the singular verb *is*.

7. **New Yorkers** with a good income **are** less likely to commute by subway.

   The prepositional phrase *with a good income* might confuse the relationship between the plural subject *New Yorkers* and the plural verb *are*.

8. A **worker** with a long commute **does** not want to spend hours on the subway.

   The singular subject *worker* takes the singular verb form *does*.

9. A **private car**, although convenient, **pollutes** the air.

   The subject *car* is singular, so it takes the singular verb form *pollutes*.

10. **Parking** in one of New York's many overcrowded garages **is** also a problem.

    The singular subject *parking* requires the singular verb *is*. Don't be misled by the plural word *garages* because it is part of a prepositional phrase, not the subject of the sentence.

11. Every day, **Joe and Carla ride** the subway to work.

    A compound subject joined by *and* is plural.

12. Every day, Joe **or Carla rides** the subway to work.

    In a compound subject joined by *or*, the verb matches the closer part of the subject. *Carla* is singular, so use the singular verb *rides*.

13. Every day, Joe's sisters **or Carla's sisters ride** the subway to work.

    In a compound subject joined by *or*, the verb matches the closer part of the subject. *Carla's sisters* is plural, so use the plural verb *ride*.

14. Every day, Joe's sisters **or Carla rides** the subway to work.

    In a compound subject joined by *or*, the verb matches the closer part of the subject. *Carla* is singular, so use the singular verb *rides*.

15. Every day, Carla **or Joe's sisters** from Long Island **ride** the subway to work.

    In a compound subject joined by *or*, the verb matches the closer part of the subject. Don't be thrown by the prepositional phrase *from Long Island*. Since *Joe's sisters* is plural, use the plural verb *ride*.

16. **Everyone enjoys** a summer vacation.

    Most indefinite pronouns, including *everyone*, are singular.

17. **Nobody has** fun when the Cyclones lose a game.

    Most indefinite pronouns, including *nobody*, are singular.

18. **Either** of the answers **is** valid in response to that question.

    Either is a singular indefinite pronoun. Disregard the prepositional phrase *of the answers* when figuring out the proper verb form.

19. **Each** of the students **brings** a book to class every day.

    Each is a singular indefinite pronoun. Disregard the prepositional phrase *of the students* when working out subject-verb agreement for this sentence.

20. **Many are** obsessed with reality television these days.

    Many is one of a very few plural indefinite pronouns in English.

Practice 3

1. The installation of video cameras in public areas certainly <u>adds</u> a measure of security but may eventually erode our right to privacy.

2. Competition for grades, jobs, and mates ultimately <u>benefits</u> society.

3. The main flaw in most of these arguments <u>is the reliance upon</u> unsupported inferences. *or* In most of these arguments, the main flaw <u>is</u> the reliance upon unsupported inferences.

Practice 4

1. The entire team of scientists <u>was</u> allergic to the very chemicals they were studying

2. [No mistake: the team as an entity can conclude work.]

3. A number of Internet companies <u>are</u> doubtless preparing to challenge Google for dominance of the search engine market.

Practice 5

1. The CEO, along with the Board of Directors, <u>is</u> responsible for any infraction of the corporation's environmental protection policy.

2. Either the Attorney General or his senior assistants <u>have</u> the option prosecuting such violations.

3. No mistake.

Practice 6

1. Looking at the data carefully, <u>we see that </u>the premises simply will not support the conclusion.

2. Having selected an appropriate brand name, <u>the entrepreneur still faces</u> many obstacles to successful marketing of the new product.

3. In this argument, an essential inference is that to pass the course <u>one must take the exam</u>.

Practice 7

1. For example, I would say that my roommate could be characterized as a poor student because he waited until the last minute to study for exams, wrote his lab reports without completing the assigned experiments, and <u>lacked motivation</u>.

2. It is reasonable for a Kravis Software sales representative to expect that he will have an opportunity to introduce his products at the meeting, that there will be a projector for his slide presentation, and <u>that</u> prospective buyers will ask questions about the product.

3. Before investing in a start-up company, the venture capitalist meets with the company's principals, reviews the business plan, <u>and evaluates</u> samples of the product or service that the company plans to offer.

Practice 8

Sentence fragments are underlined in the paragraph below:

Everyone feels shy. <u>At some point in life.</u> It is perfectly normal to be concerned about how strangers might view you in an unfamiliar situation. <u>For example, a social gathering or new job.</u> However, shyness can sometimes become a major difficulty. <u>If a person feels overpowering anxiety about common situations such as going to the store, attending classes at school, or even walking down the street.</u> That anxiety can interfere with the person's ability to carry on a normal life. A few shy people develop a serious fear of strangers. <u>Forcing them to restrict or avoid contact with people most of us interact with daily.</u> <u>Such as the mail carrier, co-workers, or teachers.</u> <u>These people who feel overwhelmed by the mere thought of contact with a stranger.</u> Such people may have agoraphobia.

One suggested way to fix the fragments in this paragraph is to connect sentences and drop words that make sentences into subordinate clauses:

Everyone feels shy at some point in life. It is perfectly normal to be concerned about how strangers might view you in an unfamiliar situation, for example, a social gathering or new job. However, shyness can sometimes become a major difficulty. If a person feels overpowering anxiety about common situations such as going to the store, attending classes at school, or even walking down the street, that anxiety can interfere with the person's ability to carry on a normal life. A few shy people develop a serious fear of strangers, forcing them to restrict or avoid contact with people most of us interact with daily, such as the mail carrier, co-workers, or teachers. These people feel overwhelmed by the mere thought of contact with a stranger. Such people may have agoraphobia.

Practice 9

1. Elementary schools must impart the tools <u>necessary to</u> teach the basic skills.

   A restrictive element ("to teach the basic skills") should not be set off by a comma.

2. The <u>role of</u> providing lifelong assistance to disabled <u>people belongs</u> to the <u>government,</u> which can muster the vast resources needed to properly care for the ill.

   The prepositional phrase "of providing . . ." is not parenthetic, so it doesn't need commas. But the nonrestrictive phrase "which can muster . . ." does need to be set off by a comma. Nonessential phrases, which begin with the word "which," are nonrestrictive.

3. Advocates of the proposed <u>law, however,</u> will most likely insist on the need to forestall improper sharing of intellectual <u>property and</u> classified information.

   The word "however," in this case, is parenthetic, so set it off with commas.

4. All the support for this argument is either flawed, superfluous or irrelevant.

   OR

   All the support for this argument is either flawed, superfluous, or irrelevant.

   Items in a series should be separated by commas. Although current usage favors omitting the last comma just before the conjunction ("or" in this case), either method is correct.

5. In fact it is just as likely that some other cause can explain why the products at the uptown factory are cheaper to produce.

   OR

   In fact, it is just as likely that some other cause can explain why the products at the uptown factory are cheaper to produce.

   The introductory clause "in fact" is short and is unlikely to cause any confusion in this sentence. Although current usage favors omitting the comma that sets off a short introductory clause, either usage is correct.

6. Although discounted, the evidence of the second survey is actually more informative to this argument.

   In this case, the comma is required even though the introductory clause is short. Without the comma, the clause "Although discounted" is likely to cause confusion as the word "discounted" runs into the first part of the subject "the evidence," that immediately follows it, so the comma is required to prevent confusion.

Practice 10

1. We may well ask ourselves what colleges can possibly do to prevent <u>cheating.</u>

2. No mistake.

3. For years, the largest contingents of international peacekeepers have come from the <u>U.K.</u> and the <u>U.S.A.</u>

Practice 11

1. When a society is in agreement on the need to meet social objectives, government generally takes on a powerful role<u>; in such cases,</u> levying taxes, rather than simply raising money, becomes, in addition, a means of implementing those goals.

2. The assets of such an enterprise might include, for example, $30 million in real estate, equipment, and <u>infrastructure; $20</u> million in cash, investments, and accounts <u>receivable; and</u> $10 million in inventory.

3. No mistake.

Practice 12

1. The prompt poses a simple question: Should the 55 mph limit be restored?

2. The question posed is, whether the 55 mph limit should be restored.

3. No mistake

Practice 13

1. Three <u>principles</u> are at issue in this case.

2. Ultimately, a leader must be guided by her <u>people's</u> wishes.

3. With very few exceptions, <u>women's</u> rights have been adjudicated by the courts over the past few <u>decades</u>.

4. Many Princes of Wales have served long terms as the heir to the crown of Great Britain, and Prince Charles's case is no exception.

Practice 14

1. In most developing <u>countries</u>, up to 80 percent of the population lives in rural <u>communities</u>.

2. No mistake.

3. <u>Humans</u> are not the only <u>primates</u> that have been known to murder their own kind: infanticide is well-documented among <u>chimpanzees</u>, <u>baboons</u>, and several species of monkeys.

Practice 15

1. In the age of electronic media, reading <u>books and magazines</u> is not as important as it once was.

2. Consumers must have the confidence that they have an option to get a <u>refund or to exchange</u> any online purchase that does not meet with their satisfaction.

3. Statistics for <u>births per year per capita</u> can give a useful measure of a nation's reproductive status.

Practice 16

(1) Abraham Lincoln described the U.S. government as being, as he said in the Gettysburg Address, "of the people, by the people, and for the people." (2) This notion, I believe, puts the priorities between the achievements of institutions and the achievements of governments in proper perspective. (3) It is not a question of the achievements of individuals vs. the achievements of the government; that contrast is a false dilemma. (4) Rather, it is the achievements of individuals, which make up the achievements of a government, that determine the greatness of a nation. (5) This is what Lincoln meant when he referred to the nation's "unfinished work": that each of us has a task to perform, and those tasks determine what kind of nation we will live in. (6) With this fundamental argument in mind, how can we not join with Lincoln in wishing that such a nation "shall not perish from the earth?"

Explanations

(1) The expression *as he said in the Gettysburg Address* is a parenthetic, and so is enclosed in commas. The quotation beginning *of the people* is a direct quotation, so it is introduced by a comma. The three items in the quote are in a series, so they should be separated by commas. Note that the comma before the conjunction in the last item *and for the people* is technically optional, although Lincoln included it in the written version of his speech so in this case it is probably best not to omit it. Also, omit the extra space between the initials of the abbreviation U.S.

(2) The phrase *I believe* is parenthetic, and so should be set off with commas. The phrase *and the achievements of government* is not parenthetic (and not in a series) so it should not be set off by commas. Omit the apostrophe on the simple plural *priorities*.

(3) This sentence is a run-on, having two independent clauses joined by a comma with no conjunction. Probably the best way to fix the run-on here is to replace the comma with a semicolon as shown (a period and new sentence would also work). Also, there's an incorrect abbreviation (with an extra space) for *versus*. Finally, omit the slash from AWA essays.

(4) The comma after the short introductory *rather* is not absolutely vital, but probably contributes to avoiding misunderstanding in this case. The nonrestrictive clause *which make up . . . government* must be set off with commas.

(5) The "unfinished work" belongs to the nation, so *nation's* takes a possessive apostrophe. The terminal colon goes outside the quotation marks. The part of the sentence after the colon consists of two independent clauses joined by a conjunction, so the clauses must be separated by a comma.

(6) The first part of this sentence, *With this fundamental . . . mind*, is a long introductory prepositional phrase, so set it off with a comma. The sentence itself is a question (beginning with *how*) so it must end with a question mark—which goes inside the quotation marks. Finally, the quote is run into the sentence, so it doesn't take an introductory comma.

Practice 17

1. During the Middle Ages and most of the Renaissance, <u>philosophy</u> was hardly distinct from <u>theology</u>.

2. By the end of <u>spring</u>, <u>American</u> and <u>Canadian</u> <u>university</u> students have been enjoying their <u>summer</u> <u>vacation</u> for well over a month.

3. Widely regarded as the most important <u>U.S.</u> <u>trade</u> <u>agreement</u> in the past two decades, the U.S.-Canada Free Trade Agreement phased out all tariffs and quotas between the two countries by the end of the twentieth century.

4. Last year, Doctor Sanford was elected president of the Brooklyn council The president of the council meets regularly with the Dean of Students.

5. American Independence Day and Memorial Day occur during the summer, but Labor Day is in the fall.

6. The novels of William Faulkner are set in the American South, and the author himself lived most of his life south of the Mason-Dixon Line.

Practice 18

Many people think it is **all right** to **accept** public assistance **regardless** of their ability to secure financial **independence** for themselves. Other people think it **cannot affect** them, or that they do not **lose** money, if these **professional** charity cases force the government to **accommodate their** free **rein**. I would not be **exaggerating** if I said that **no one** lives in a **vacuum**, and all **decent** people need to be **responsible** for **their** own welfare **too**. I **wonder** if it would **have** ever **occurred to** these folks to **assent** to **buy** food, clothing, and shelter firsthand for people who will not **alter** their **indiscreet** financial habits. I think **it's** unlikely. When **you're** looking **past** the question of **who's** paying for these goods and services, **then you're accepting their** right to **steal** from **your** pocket **every day**.

Practice 19

1. In fields such as human <u>development</u> and family <u>planning</u>, it is <u>becoming</u> easier to find funding for basic research.

2. As the hailstorm intensified, the campers <u>panicked</u> and ran <u>screaming</u> through the grounds.

3. No mistake.

Practice 20

1. <u>It's [or: It is]</u> often necessary to <u>buy</u> more goods <u>than</u> can be consumed in a single day even though <u>they're [they are]</u> likely to spoil.

2. I would <u>have</u> thought that journalists should avoid taking sides when they <u>write</u> about such controversial subjects.

3. We all <u>hear</u> stories of people <u>whose</u> children refuse to accompany them on vacations.

4. Can you <u>cite</u> three <u>incidents</u> in the <u>past</u> in which Congress has given its <u>assent</u> to such a proposal?

5. The board of education <u>accepted</u> the <u>advice</u> of the high school <u>principal</u> in <u>choosing</u> to <u>alter</u> the wording of the teachers' contracts.

6. After years of suffering under the <u>heel</u> of an autocrat, the citizens must <u>steel</u> themselves for change.

Practice 21

1. <u>Many people</u> are <u>obsessed with</u> video games and <u>television, which I believe are relatively harmless wastes of time.</u>

2. These days there are many reality shows, <u>such as *Survivor* and *American Idol*, that are all essentially similar.</u>

3. <u>Often</u> a perfectly good plan can be <u>ruined</u> by a minor oversight.

Practice 22

Your version may vary.

It is supportable to argue that studying an academic discipline changes your view of the world. For example, if you study history, you often read about many facts that are as important as the ones you learned about in school, but which weren't covered. Many large social trends and beliefs that you think are valid today turn out to be wrong. Studying a discipline such as history can change how you look at the world.

Practice 23

1. A surge of power destroyed the coolant pumps.

2. A bolt of lightning struck the transformer.

3. The slow goalkeeper failed to stop the ball.

4. Manic-depressives experience unpredictable moods.

KAPLAN

5. The administrative secretary monitors and balances the budgets.

6. Hikers must remain on marked trails.

7. All too often, our coaches have recruited athletes with marginal academic skills.

8. The media portrays or stereotypes teachers as illiterate, even though they fulfill strict requirements.

Practice 24

Simple	Sometimes the fresh perspective of a nonexpert can be valuable in the consideration of a subject.
Compound	Experts often have the best advice about a subject, but sometimes the fresh perspective of a nonexpert can be valuable too.
Complex	Although experts often have the best advice about a subject, sometimes the fresh perspective of a nonexpert can be valuable too.
Compound-Complex	Because experts typically have the most information about a subject, they often have the best advice about that subject, but sometimes the fresh perspective of a nonexpert can be valuable too.

Simple	The tangible rewards of society are at least as important as the feeling of having fulfilled a personal goal.
Compound	The feeling of having fulfilled a personal goal is important, but the tangible rewards of society are at least as important.
Complex	Although the feeling of having fulfilled a personal goal is important, the tangible rewards of society are at least as important.
Compound-Complex	Rewards are important, and although the feeling of having fulfilled a personal goal is important, the tangible rewards of society are at least as important.

Simple	The important question is whether the combined cost of pest control and savings in product damage are greater with Company B.
Compound	The important question is not which pest-control company is cheaper, but rather which company provides the best combination of cost and savings in product damage.
Complex	Even though Company B is more expensive, the important question is whether the combined cost of pest control and savings in product damage are greater with Company B.
Compound-Complex	Even though Company B is more expensive, if the combined cost of pest control and savings due to product damage is greater, then Company B is a better deal overall.

Simple	It is an oversimplification to say that there can be no meaningful interaction between academic communities with different traditions.
Compound	Different academic communities have different traditions, but it is an oversimplification to say that these differences preclude meaningful interaction between them.
Complex	Even though different academic communities may have different traditions, it is an oversimplification to say that there can be no meaningful interaction between them.
Compound-Complex	Different academic communities have different traditions, and while these differences may be significant, it is an oversimplification to say that there can be no meaningful interaction between them.

Simple	It is reasonable to argue that a cheaper brand of sunscreen might encourage people to have a false sense of security.
Compound	The cheaper brand of sunscreen is less effective, and so the sense of security it gives is false.
Complex	Because the cheaper brand of sunscreen is less effective, it is certainly reasonable to say that it encourages a false sense of security.
Compound-Complex	Because the cheaper brand of sunscreen is less effective, and because it encourages people to stay in the sun longer, it is fair to say that it encourages a false sense of security.

Practice 25

Answers will vary slightly.

Repetitive words and phrases in this paragraph: *courses, development, job market*

Synonyms for "courses": *lessons, classes, curricula, programs, learning, education*

Synonyms for "development": *improvement, training, education, advancement, enhancement*

Synonyms for "job market": *employment, professional setting, occupation, trade, the world of work*

Sample rewrite using these synonyms:

A curriculum that focuses on intellectual improvement is more important than a curriculum that contributes to professional training. An educational program that emphasizes professional advancement assumes that this education will still be relevant to the future occupation of the student, while in fact the constant changes in the job market might make such learning obsolete. In contrast, a course of study that works toward intellectual growth trains a person for a variety of occupational roles, so that even if the demands of employers change, the educational program remains relevant. This is not to say that many curricula cannot do both: preparing a person for employment in a specific field while also preparing her for a variety of potential vocations. But, while classes that provide professional training have their place in the realm of university curricula, they should not be allowed to supersede education that trains the intellect for the ever-changing world of work.

Chapter 3: **Writing Strong Essays on Test Day**

In this chapter, we'll review the writing process and the steps you need to take to produce a top-notch LSAT Writing Sample. We'll also review the logic skills you need to effectively present arguments. Finally, we'll show you the Kaplan Four-Step Method for the Writing Sample as well as templates to use on test day.

PART ONE: THE WRITING PROCESS

You probably know by now that a good written *product* comes from a good writing *process*. Whether you tend to brainstorm and organize in your head or put everything down on paper, whether you like to write one draft or ten, your writing will come out stronger when you start with a **plan**, **write** out your ideas, and then **revise** and **edit** your work.

In most real-life writing situations, you have plenty of time to work through each of these writing stages. For the LSAT Writing Sample, however, you only have 35 minutes. So, should you just forget about the planning stage and jump right in to the essay?

Absolutely not. Even though your time is limited, even if you tend to write well under pressure, you're far more likely to write a persuasive argument if you work through each stage of the writing process (especially the planning stage). A few minutes of brainstorming can help you come up with powerful examples to support your position; a few minutes of revising and editing can help you catch and correct errors that would otherwise detract from your essay. So here's a review of the writing process as it specifically applies to writing a clear, concise and persuasive argument in your LSAT Writing Sample.

Planning Your Essay

This first step in the writing process is also perhaps the most essential for a timed essay exam. Planning (also called **prewriting**) should take about five to seven minutes of your test time (save about 25 minutes for the actual writing, and another three to five minutes for revising and editing).

Understand the Scenario

Before brainstorming, before outlining, before you do anything else, make sure you understand the scenario and the two possible courses of action. Read the material carefully and as many times as you need to.

The prompt presents a scenario and then describes two choices. Either choice can be supported based on the information provided. You need to consider both choices and then argue for one choice over the other, keeping in mind the specific criteria outlined. It is important that you remember that there is no right or wrong choice and that an effective argument can be made for either course of action.

For example, let's look at a sample prompt:

"Play it Again," a used sports equipment store owned and operated by Louis and Angie Peters, has been located at the same downtown site for six years. However, the Peters must move the store when their lease terminates next month. They are considering two possible locations. Write an argument for one of the two following choices. Two considerations should influence your decision:

- The Peters hope to minimize the time and expense involved in restarting their business in a new location.

- The Peters seek maximum potential for business growth and for return on their financial investment.

The Peters are considering a location on Bloom Court where a pet store has recently failed. The Bloom Court storefront is only a few blocks away from the Peters' present location. Although the space would be just large enough to support the Peters' current operation, they could expand to an adjacent retail space in the same building. While the Peters' present location is on a busy, primarily commercial street, Bloom Court is a quiet side-street lined with charming row houses and a few neighborhood stores. Most Bloom Court residents are either recent retirees or young couples in their twenties.

The Peters are also considering a location in the Town and Country suburban mall, which is approximately four miles from their current location. The space, which is situated across from the mall's food court, is large enough for the Peters' current and potential future needs. The monthly rent is a little less than twice that of the Bloom Court location. Although parking at the mall is ample, there is only limited public transportation between the mall and the downtown area.

Before you choose which location to support, consider the pros and cons of both locations. Make sure that you fully understand the considerations that you need to keep in mind when making a choice. In this case, you must show how your choice will meet the specified criteria: to help the Peters "to minimize the time and expense involved in restarting their business in a new location" while providing "maximum potential for business growth and for return on their financial investment."

Brainstorm Ideas

Now that your task is clear, it's time to start brainstorming ideas. Do you know what position you want to take from the get-go, or do you need to think about it? Think it through on paper.

Brainstorming Techniques *Brainstorming* simply refers to the technique of focusing on a particular problem or issue to come up with ideas. For an essay, you can try **listing** or **free writing.** Write down whatever comes to your mind about the topic. Remember that in a brainstorm, *anything goes.* Don't discount any ideas yet—you're still in the planning stage, and an idea that doesn't seem relevant now can lead you to another that may form the crux of your argument. Forget about grammar, sentence structure, or anything else that might hinder your thoughts. Just get your ideas down on paper. If you know as soon as you read the decision prompt what position you would like to argue, then jump right into the second step: brainstorming support for your argument. It's particularly important to brainstorm ideas for opposing points of view so you can address counterarguments in your essay.

Below are examples of these brainstorming techniques for the sample "Play it Again" decision prompt.

Listing means just that—simply list whatever ideas come to mind. In the sample list below, the author listed the pros and cons of each location.

Bloom Court

— Pros

Close to current location – existing customers won't have to travel far.

Low rent

Moving expenses may be lower

Space can grow with the business

— Cons

Less traffic than existing location

Prior business failed

Town and Country Mall

— Pros

Parking

Prime location next to food court

Large space

— Cons

Space may be too large to begin with

High rent

Limited public transportation

May lose current customers who don't want to travel to mall

Free writing is exactly that—a free narrative response to develop ideas unencumbered by the conventions of essay writing (no worries about grammar, paragraphing, cohesion, etc.).

Bloom Ct may be too residential and the residents don't seem like the type of customers that the store would court. But, maybe retirees start playing sports with their free time and the young couples could be very active. A sports store doesn't have to be just for kids. Maybe the demographics would be right on. A quiet street means less competition. But is there parking? Being close to the original storefront means that regular customers wouldn't feel like Play it Again is completely uprooting and leaving the downtown – there could be patrons who are anti-mall and only support downtown businesses. Plus, the lower rent will help minimize expense. The Peters would have to do more marketing to current customers if they move to the mall. But, being across from the food court means high visibility. Are people in buying mode when they stop for food? When I'm at the mall I sometimes pass by the stores next to the food. Not sure whether that is a pro or con. Also what if the mall space is too big for them? Will they have to invest in additional inventory to fill the space at the same time as they are incurring all the moving expenses and the higher rent? At Bloom Ct, they could enlarge the store only if they need to – it would be an option and they could do it on their schedule.

Outline Your Essay

Once you've brainstormed ideas, it's time to put them—quickly—into a logical order. It might be tempting to just jump in and write, but resist that temptation. A good outline will make the actual writing of your essay much easier and help minimize revising needs. At the LSAT, you will be given scratch paper so you can plan your essay before writing it on the Writing Sample Response Sheet.

The goal of an outline is twofold: (1) to put the ideas you brainstormed into a logical order and (2) to help ensure that you have enough support for the course of action you plan to support in your essay. By laying everything out before you write, you can see if you have any gaps in support or logic in your argument. If so, you can fix those problems before it's too late. You can also map out a logical sequence of ideas so that your argument flows smoothly from one paragraph to another.

USING SCRATCH PAPER

On test day, you will be provided with scratch paper to use for outlining your essay. Be sure that you **do not** use the scratch paper for your actual essay. Anything you write on the scratch paper will not be considered part of your essay and, therefore, will not be reproduced to be sent to the law schools along with your LSAT score.

A Well-Organized Outline = Well-Organized Essay   You may tend to resist writing outlines for your normal writing tasks, but on a timed exam like the LSAT it is an important step. Outlining your essay will make the actual writing part of your essay go more quickly. Also, it will help you to organize your thoughts so you can produce an organized essay.

At the broadest level, the essay must have a beginning, a middle, and an end. The first paragraph must state your position. The body of the essay must present two to four well-developed points in support of the claim staked out in the introduction. The conclusion should summarize the essay as a whole.

Too often, though, this three-part structure becomes something of a "list sandwich": the introduction and conclusion are just there to hold an undifferentiated list of points. As a result, the reader has no idea where the argument is going and feels jerked along, rather than feeling like a paying customer on a guided tour. While it is not necessary to declare explicitly the rationale behind your organization, you should definitely lay out your points in a clear trajectory. That is, your supporting ideas must be arranged in some logical sequence, even if there is no logical necessity to that sequence.

You're in luck with the LSAT Writing Sample. You already know the structure of your essay topic so you can decide in advance how you will structure your response. By deciding on your structure before the exam, there will be one less factor for you to consider on test day. Here, we'll examine two of the most common formats for the Writing Sample. Either one would work well for presenting an argument.

The first option is the "winner/loser" format. In this format, the first paragraph begins with a statement of choice and then discusses all of the reasons your choice (the winner) is superior. The next paragraph focuses on why the other alternative (the loser) is not as good. The conclusion can be its own paragraph or simply a sentence or two at the end of the second paragraph. Either way, the conclusion should reaffirm your decision.

The second option is the "according to the criteria" format. This format should begin the same at the "winner/loser" format, with a statement declaring which course of action you have chosen. The difference is that after the declaration, the first paragraph would discuss both the winner and the loser in light of the first criterion. The second paragraph would discuss them both in light of the second criterion. Your conclusion would stand as the final paragraph, again reaffirming your decision.

While we have found these formats are easy to use on test day, you may wish to use your own. That's perfectly acceptable. The most important thing for you to keep in mind when deciding on a structure is that your essay must be coherent in its reasoning. The more organized your essay is, the more persuasive it will be.

Once you've determined your overall organizing principle, outline your major supporting points and the specific evidence and examples you can use to support each of those main points. Here's an example of the "winner/loser" format using the "Play it Again" decision prompt:

1. Intro: Bloom Ct is the better location for the Peters.

    a. minimal moving expenses

    b. uninterrupted business for customers

    c. low initial rent, ensure short term survival

    d. long term growth when needed – Peters can save money for expansion at later date

2.   Town and Country Mall not ideal

    a.   high traffic from prime location might seem better for long term growth

    b.   high rent could off-set any growth making short term survival difficult

    c.   the space may initially be too large

    d.   need to court new customers because location is not easily accessible from downtown

Conclusion: reaffirm position

A Well-Developed Outline = A Well-Developed Essay   Why is *development* an issue in the outlining stage? Because your outline can show you which paragraphs need more support. Now's the time to review your outline for completeness. Do you have enough ideas and information to cover each topic thoroughly? Do you cover everything you need to cover, including counterarguments?

Writing Your Essay

Now that you have a detailed outline, the actual writing of your essay should go rather smoothly. You know what you want to say and the order in which you want to say it.

Introductions: Get off to a Strong Start

In regular academic writing, your essay introductions typically have two main goals: (1) to grab the reader's attention and (2) to clearly state your thesis or position. On the LSAT Writing Sample, however, your focus should emphatically be on the latter. Right from the start, readers need to know which course of action your essay will support. The first sentence of your essay should immediately offer a statement of your position. Do not waste time and space describing the scenario; assume that your readers are familiar with the situation.

What about grabbing the reader's attention with a catchy introduction? The Writing Sample is not the place. On the LSAT, you don't have time to waste thinking of a good attention-grabber, so stick to a standard introduction. Save your creativity for your personal statement.

Writing Strong Paragraphs

A paragraph by definition is a group of sentences about a single idea. Make sure your paragraphs have clear topic sentences stating that main idea of each paragraph. In your regular writing you may be more subtle, but for the LSAT Writing Sample you want to be as clear and obvious as possible.

Developing Ideas   There's no magic number for how many sentences should be in a paragraph, because this depends on the length of sentences and the purpose of the paragraph. For example, there are times when a short, one-sentence paragraph is rhetorically effective.

To play it safe on the exam, aim for three-to-five-sentence paragraphs throughout your essay. In general, that's about what it takes, given average sentence lengths, to fully develop an idea: one topic sentence, two or three sentences with specific examples or evidence, and a sentence or two acknowledging and refuting counterarguments or providing a transition into the next paragraph.

The only exception to this guideline for paragraph length might be the conclusion, which is likely to be more concise than other paragraphs because there isn't a new idea to develop.

Organizing Ideas   You've already decided upon your overall principle of organization in your outline. But an effective essay includes not just macro-organization (overall organizing principle of the essay), but also meso- (intermediate, paragraph level) and micro- (sentence level) organization as well. At the meso-scale, there are three issues:

1. **Paragraph unity.** Does each paragraph deal with a single coherent idea? Do any extraneous ideas creep in to distract the reader's attention? Remember that your essay should focus only on the information provided in the decision prompt. Writing off-topic is unacceptable. Your readers will catch off-topic sentences no matter how quickly they read through your essay.

2. **Topic sentences.** Does each paragraph have one main idea clearly stated in a topic sentence? We all know that the topic sentence can occur anywhere in the paragraph. Perfectly good paragraphs may even lack a topic sentence. But on the exam, play it safe. If at all possible, deploy a fully developed topic sentence at the opening of each paragraph.

3. **Transitional phrases.** Are there smooth and effective transitions between and within paragraphs? Your entire essay should be stitched together with transitional phrases. From the second paragraph to the conclusion, each topic sentence should begin with a conspicuous signpost marking the trajectory of your argument: *the first problem, first of all, second, furthermore, one additional factor, in conclusion,* etc. Within each paragraph, use signals that will draw the reader's attention to what you are doing: *such as, for example, an alternative explanation, on the one hand/on the other, by contrast, however, nonetheless, consequently, therefore,* and so on.

Here's a more complete list of some of the most useful transitional words and phrases for your essays:

Purpose	Transitions
show addition	and, also, again, in addition, furthermore, moreover, besides, next, too
introduce an example	for example, for instance, such as, in particular, in fact, in other words, that is, specifically, on the one hand/other, to illustrate
indicate the passage of time	before, after, afterward, next, during, meanwhile, later, eventually, in the meantime, immediately, suddenly, finally
indicate rank	first, second, third, etc. (of all); first and foremost; most important; more importantly; above all
indicate cause	because, since, for this reason
indicate effect	as a result, consequently, therefore, hence
indicate comparison	similarly, likewise, like, just as, in the same manner
indicate contrast	but, however, on the other hand, on the contrary, conversely, in contrast, yet, whereas, instead, rather, while, although, though, despite
to add emphasis	in fact, indeed, certainly, above all,
to summarize or conclude	in sum, in summary, in short, in conclusion, to conclude, to sum up, that is, therefore

DEVELOPMENT AND ORGANIZATION

A well-**developed** Writing Sample:

- has three to four full paragraphs.
- has at least three sentences in each paragraph, with the possible exception of a concise conclusion.
- provides specific examples, details, or evidence for the main idea of each paragraph.

A well-**organized** Writing Sample:

- has an overall organizing principle for the essay.
- has an organizing principle for each paragraph.
- has only one main idea per paragraph.
- clearly states the main idea of each paragraph.
- has strong transitions between sentences and between paragraphs.

Wrapping It All Up: Writing Your Conclusion

Think for a moment about the last movie you saw. What's the first scene that comes to mind? Chances are you remember best the beginning or the end of the film. For better or for worse, first and final impressions really count, and this is especially true in writing. Indeed, conclusions often have the power to make or break an essay. A weary admissions counselor, for example, might be well satisfied throughout your essay only to be disappointed by a particularly weak conclusion.

As we've said many times now, your best bet is to play it safe throughout your essay, and this includes the conclusion. You want your ending to have impact, but you don't have the time or the rhetorical freedom to anything fancy with your conclusion. Instead, stick to a standard conclusion that:

1. restates *your* main idea *and*

2. *briefly* summarizes your main support.

Your conclusion should *not*:

- Repeat your position in exactly the same words. Your essay is too short for direct repetition. When you restate your main idea, make sure it's an effective paraphrase.

- Open a new can of worms. A good conclusion will always provide a sense of closure for readers so that they feel as if the topic has been covered completely. If you introduce a new topic, readers will feel cheated because your essay is over and you have no place to develop this new idea.

STAY POSITIVE!

Sweaty palms. Pounding heart. Self-defeating internal thoughts. On test day, you might not be able to stop your palms from sweating and your heart from pounding rapidly – you're sure to be nervous after all. But, you can stop those self-defeating thoughts. If you find yourself thinking things like, "I'll never be able to write a cogent essay in 35 minutes," or, "I'm getting so tired and stressed that I won't be able to develop an argument to save my life," you can turn it around. Remember that by reading this book and completing the exercises you have taken a big step toward ensuring that you are well prepared for the LSAT Writing Sample. You will enter the LSAT exam supported by a four-step plan for writing a winning essay and refreshed writing and logic skills. So, feel confident and replace your self-defeating and negative thoughts with positive ones. You can do it!

Revising and Editing Your Essay

The difference between *revising* and *editing* is simple: revising refers to any changes you make above and beyond the level of grammar and usage, mechanics, or formatting, as these are the realm of editing. Typically writers are advised to revise first, as revision addresses big-picture issues such as organization and development and sentence-level issues such as structure and word choice. But your time on the LSAT Writing Sample is limited, and if you used your time effectively, you will only have about three to five minutes left to review your essay. So you will have to revise and edit simultaneously.

Big Picture Checklist

As you revise, check for the following "big picture" issues. Your essay should:

- **State ideas assertively and clearly.** Do you clearly state your position at the beginning of your essay? Do you have clear topic sentences in each paragraph?

- **Develop ideas fully.** Do you explain your ideas clearly and completely? Do you provide strong and specific support for your argument?

- **Organize ideas logically.** Do you have an effective organizing principle for your essay? Within your paragraphs? Have you paragraphed effectively?

- **Stay focused.** Does your essay stick to one main idea? Is all of your support relevant? Are your paragraphs free from any sentences that are off-topic?

- **Signpost constantly.** Do you use strong transitions within and between paragraphs?

Sentence-Level Checklist

On the sentence level, check for the Eight Maxims of Effective Writing:

- Are your sentences **correct**? Can you find and correct any errors in grammar or mechanics?

- Are your sentences **clear**? Are there any ambiguous or vague sentences because of poor sentence structure or word choice?

- Are your sentences **concise**? Can you eliminate any unnecessary repetition or wordiness?

- Are your sentences **exact**? Have you used exact words and phrases as well as specific details?

- Are your sentences **assertive**? Do you state your points without hesitation?

- Are your sentences **appropriate**? Do you use the right level of formality throughout your essay?

- Are your sentences **consistent**? Do you maintain an appropriate style, tone, and point of view throughout your essay?

- Are your sentences **exciting**? Do you have variety in sentence structure and vocabulary?

Chapter 2 covers each of the eight maxims in greater detail. Review that chapter if you find your sentences are not consistently effective.

Practice 1

Directions: Each paragraph includes numerous errors of the types covered in this book. Practice proofreading by locating and correcting all the errors in each paragraph. Compare your answers to the answers starting on page 114.

Paragraph 1

(1) The advise given to the company managers that hiring more additional workers will result in a larger number of houses being built contain a fallacy of exclusion. (2) Several pieces of extremely vital information are not taken into consideration in the reasoning that more workers means more houses built, a moments reasoning reveals that many factors other then merely the number of workers determines the answer to the question of how many houses will be built? (3) For example, if the construction company doesn't have enough construction equipment/tools to equip more worker's, then extra workers won't help irregardless. (4) If there aren't enough building sights available, a raw materials shortage, or sufficient infrastructure to support additional workers, then hiring more workers might well been just a waste of money. (5) The whole question of diminishing returns is not considered by this line of reasoning at all in increasing staff size.

Paragraph 2

(1) While the School Boards argument that eating breakfast is related to a reduction of absenteeism in the school breakfast program may be convincing. (2) The conclusion that forcing more students to eat breakfast on the school program will cause a decreasing drop in absences is unwarranted. (3) The statistic's show a correspondance that is far from clear enough to assume causation. (4) The attendance of students at the school-sponsored breakfast program and at subsequent classes maybe both result from a third, unexamined cause that creates the observed affect. (5) For example, students who eat school breakfasts everyday might just happen to be the ones who go to bed early, and therefore are up in time for both the breakfast and for classes. (6) Or maybe the students with better attendance experience a different kind of parent supervision that contributes to both one's better diet and their improved attendance.

Paragraph 3

(1) In surveying their customers and found that they prefer games with lifelike graphics, the computer game company has correctly identified a cause for an increase in the popularity of particular game types. (2) From the evidence presented it seems okay to think that certain customers might maybe buy the more lifelike games in preference to games with worse graphics. (3) However, the conclusion that game sales will rise as an end result of this action neglects to take into account the evidence. (4) That the more lifelike games require the latest new computer hardware. (5) The argument presents no evidence to show the fact that the target audience is undergoing a transition to this more advanced and more expensive type of computer platform. On the contrary common sense seems perhaps to suggest that, since the target audience tends to be young, that their earning power would not allow them to acquire the equipment necessary to accomodate the games in question, and thus it would not necessarily result in increased sales of those games. (7) If the company was to invest in developement of these games, they might waste money in the end.

PART TWO: A BRIEF LOGIC PRIMER

Logic is a key factor in writing an effective argument, which is what you will be asked to do on the LSAT Writing Sample. Admissions officers are, of course, looking for logical organization in your essays. Equally important, they are looking for logic in your argument in support of your position.

A quick primer in some of the basics of critical thinking, including the basic structure of arguments and common logical fallacies, will give you a real edge in preparing for and writing an effective essay on test day. Use the practices provided to hone your ability to recognize logical fallacies so that you can feel confident that your essay will present a sound argument.

Basic Argument Structure

First, some terms. In logic, an **argument** is not a quarrel, dispute, or verbal disagreement. Rather, it is a persuasive appeal involving two or more statements, including a **conclusion** and at least one **premise** (evidence to support that conclusion). A conclusion is the main claim of the argument. The conclusion of an argument may take the form of a declarative statement, but it may also be embedded in a proposal, recommendation, plan, or prediction. It is only a conclusion *as part of* an argument; without the premise(s) to support it, it is simply an **assertion** or **claim** that lacks support.

LOGIC TERMS

Claim: an assertion that is either true or false

Argument: a set of claims with a premise(s) and conclusion

Conclusion: the main claim of the argument

Premise: claims that support the conclusion

Premises and Conclusions

When you write your essay, you will be arguing in support of one course of action. Your argument will include a set of claims with a premise, or premises, and a conclusion. There are several words and phrases that are typically used to indicate premises and conclusions.

Common words used to indicate a **conclusion** include:

therefore	this proves/shows/suggests/implies that
so	we can infer that
hence	which implies that
thus	should
accordingly	must
consequently	may be inferred from
it follows that	

Common verbal indicators of a **premise** include:

because

since

in as much as

given that

for the following reasons

in view of the fact that

Logical Fallacies

Your task in the essay is to show why one of the two possible courses of action is better than the other. You will need to support your position and express the weaknesses of the other option. As you build your argument, you should beware of making leaps in logic, developing erroneous assumptions, and using vague or otherwise problematic terms. Doing so will detract from your argument. Common sense alone will often be enough to identify these faults and help you steer clear of them. But when under pressure you may not be aware that what seems at first to be logical may actually be a logical fallacy. Thus, we provide a brief review of the most common of those fallacies.

False Dilemma

False dilemma is one of the fundamental fallacies in logic. A familiar example of this fallacy is "America: love it or leave it." This statement assumes that there are only two options: love America or leave it—and we must choose only between these two courses of action. Obviously, there are other options: we might love some things about America, but not everything; we might not love it, but choose to stay anyway; and so on. Hence this is a false dilemma, because there are more than two options from which to choose. Watch out for using statements that present a false dilemma in your Writing Sample.

Practice 2

Each of the following presents a false dilemma. Prove that the dilemma is false by listing alternatives in the space provided. Answers are found on page 116.

1. The key to success is not competition but cooperation.

   _____

   _____

   _____

2. The goal of an educational system must be to instill values, not to provide vocational training.

   _____

   _____

   _____

3. Government needs to provide social services instead of wasting money on the arts.

   _____

   _____

   _____

4. If you're not going to work hard at your job, you should quit.

   _____

   _____

   _____

5. Anybody who supported that bill in the Senate either didn't understand the issue or was trying to ruin America.

   _____

   _____

   _____

6. The challenger is so unskilled in chess that the champion will either lose the game and be humiliated, or win and feel really guilty.

   _____

   _____

   _____

Overstated Generalization

Overstated generalizations are fairly easy to catch. Often such propositions make a broad statement about a specific group or institution:

Professional athletes must take their responsibility as role models more seriously.

Government cannot support the arts without undermining them.

It is not the place of schools to provide health education.

Other signs of the overstated generalization are superlatives (*the most important*), and extreme adverbs (*never, always, rarely, only, everything, nothing, impossible,* and of course *extremely*):

The chief lesson of history is that we have nothing to learn from it.

Progress arises only out of disagreement and discontent.

In terms of both form and content, these stimuli are frequently aphoristic: like proverbs, they are rhetorically balanced, morally instructive, and somewhat paradoxical. Here's a perfect example:

Success is easy to achieve but difficult to enjoy.

Statements like this often *sound* sound. But the problem is that they make assumptions about the whole when there is at least one possible exception to the statement. For example, don't some people enjoy their success? Don't some people (in fact, probably many) have a difficult time achieving success? In reality, these overstated generalizations are much like false dilemmas—they assume only X is true and don't consider alternatives. False dilemmas present you with two choices; you have to think of the in-betweens. Overstated generalizations state one point of view; again, you have to think of the alternatives.

You should avoid overstated generalizations in your essay. In your haste to support your position, you may find yourself making one but it is important that you pay attention to what you are writing and avoid overstated generalizations.

Practice 3

Each of the following presents an overstated generalization. Prove that the generalization is overstated by listing exceptions in the space provided. Answers are found on page 117.

1. Government should never seek to restrict the rights of individuals.

   _____

   _____

   _____

2. In business, the most important secret to success is originality.

   _____

   _____

   _____

3. In leadership, no skill is so rare and yet so vital as the ability to make decisions.

   _____

   _____

   _____

4. Any person who thinks schoolteachers have an easy job wouldn't last a day in most public schools.

   _____

   _____

   _____

5. The main goal of research should be practical technology that makes life more enjoyable for people in general.

   _____

   _____

   _____

6. In today's society, everyone thinks that style is more important than substance.

   _____

   _____

   _____

Appeal to Authority

In making an argument, it is frequently legitimate to invoke the views of authorities. The argument might be strong if the authorities have pertinent expertise and credibility. The argument will be less strong if it cites "experts" without establishing their credentials or if there is substantial disagreement among experts as to the point in question. An argument based on anonymous authority (like one based on hearsay) is extremely weak, since the expertise of the authority cannot be verified.

For example, the following is an appeal to authority:

> Experts agree that to an overwhelming extent . . .

Who are these experts? What are there credentials? A serious flaw in an argument that starts this way is that it doesn't provide credentials for these authorities. The evidence attributed to anonymous experts may seem unobjectionable, but the appeal to authority is itself a weakness in the argument and should be avoided in your essay.

Inductive Fallacies

Inductive reasoning frequently involves drawing inferences about a population as a whole based on information about a sample. Inductive fallacies arise from inappropriate reliance on a sample. That is, the conclusion is drawn from a sample that is too small (hasty generalization), unrepresentative of the target population (unrepresentative sample), or not analogous to the target population (false analogy).

Practice 4

The following is an example of inductive reasoning. Identify the conclusion and premises. Is the conclusion valid? Is it true? Answers are found on page 117.

The following appeared in a memo from a member of the school board in the town of Delos.

> "For the past five years, Mr. Evan Brockhoff has been the head football coach at Central High School. During that time the varsity football team from Central High has won three state championships. In addition, the quality of the gymnasium and the athletic equipment at Central High has improved significantly over the past five years. Because of the outstanding achievements of Central High, the Delos school board should hire Mr. Brockoff as the general director in charge of athletic programs for the entire Delos school system."

Conclusion:

_____

_____

_____

_____

_____

_____

_____

_____

_____

Premises:

_____

_____

_____

_____

_____

_____

_____

_____

_____

Hasty Generalization

A hasty generalization occurs when the size of the sample is too small to serve as a basis for the conclusion. We make hasty generalizations all the time. Eat at a restaurant once, for example, and say the food is lousy—hasty generalization. Eat at it two or three times, trying different dishes each time, and you have a better sample upon which to make your judgment.

The following is an example of a hasty generalization:

> Surveillance cameras installed in two of the town's ten municipal parking lots show that the lots are overcrowded, particularly between 8:30–10:00, 11:30–1:00, and 4:00–5:30. Overcrowded lots during these periods create hazards to drivers and pedestrians and increase congestion in nearby streets. Therefore, to alleviate congestion and improve safety, the township needs to build a new, multilevel municipal parking garage.

Common sense should tell you that two out of ten is not a large enough sample to come to the conclusion about all the parking lots in this argument. These two lots may be busier than the other eight—we don't know—and we can't rely on the information from this small a sample.

When you are preparing your argument for the Writing Sample, make sure that you don't base your support on hasty generalizations.

Unrepresentative Sample

An unrepresentative sample is one that differs in significant ways from the population as a whole. For example, if a study of sleep disorders is conducted on teenagers, but the results are projected on the entire population (including children and the elderly), the argument is invalid because the conclusions are based on an unrepresentative sample. Teenagers are a specific group within the population with specific characteristics that are not shared by other segments of the population. Likewise, the two parking lots in the hasty generalization sample stimulus might not be representative of the parking lots as a group. They may be much busier, or significantly smaller, or differ in other important ways from the other eight lots.

False Analogy   In making an analogy, one first establishes that two entities, processes, or situations are similar; then one infers that since the first term of comparison has a certain property; that property must also occur in the second term. A false analogy (comparing apples to oranges) occurs when the two terms of comparison differ in such a way as to invalidate the inferred commonality. For example:

> Our mall franchise has 30 percent less seating than our downtown franchise, yet it produces nearly twice the daily revenue. The lack of seating often creates a crowded condition in the store. This gives passersby the impression that our products are highly desirable. If we want to increase in our downtown franchise, we should cut back on seating.

There are many problems with the logic in this argument, but the most fundamental is that the two franchises are not directly comparable because of their locations. Mall traffic is likely to be heavier and steadier than a typical downtown location.

Practice 5

In what way is the sample in the following excerpt unrepresentative of the population about which the claim is made? Answer is found on page 118.

Typically, as people age, the fatty deposits in their blood vessels (atherosclerosis) increase in size and number, making people more vulnerable to blood clots and blockages. A recent study concludes an effective way to reduce the risk of blockages in later life is to take aspirin daily. The four-year study followed a group of Belgian women in their eighties who were residents of assisted care facilities. The women were given daily dosages of aspirin. In addition, the women participated in an aquatic aerobics program. After three years, these women showed a much lower rate of atherosclerosis than is average for their age.

Ways the sample is unrepresentative:

_____

_____

_____

Practice 6

Identify the analogy and explain its weakness. Answer is found on page 118.

When Stuckley's Family Buffet first opened, it was the largest, most heavily attended restaurant in town. It is still the largest restaurant, but it is no longer heavily used. A tally of table receipts last month revealed Stuckley's Buffet's drop in popularity: the receipts showed an average of only 50 parties of diners per day. In contrast, tiny Javamunch Cafe in the heart of the business district is visited by more than 150 people on a typical weekday. An obvious difference is that Javamunch Café, unlike Stuckley's Buffet, provides full table service instead of buffet-style dining. Thus, if Stuckley's Buffet is ever to be as popular as Javamunch, the management will obviously need to provide full table service, thereby providing what customers want.

Analogy:

_____

_____

_____

Weaknesses:

_____

_____

_____

Causal Fallacies

Post Hoc, Ergo Propter Hoc   The easiest causal fallacy to identify is probably *post hoc, ergo propter hoc* ("after this, therefore because of this"). The fallacious assumption is that because X came before Y, it *caused* Y. However, there are three other important possibilities:

X and Y might have independent causes

X and Y might have the same cause

X might have been only one of several causes.

Here's an example:

> Our mall franchise put a new coat of paint on the walls, purchased potted plants, and put fresh flowers on the tables to coincide with the launch of our new value menu. In the first week of the new menu, its sales were 20 percent higher than all other franchises, and on many customer satisfaction surveys, clients specifically mentioned the new décor. To increase business at our other franchises, we should similarly upgrade the décor.

Of course, the improved décor came before the launch of the new menu, but it's not likely the décor alone is responsible for the significantly higher percentage of sales. It certainly may be a factor, but there are too many other possible factors, including the knowns—the new value menu and the high-traffic location—and possible unknowns, such as advertising.

Indeed, in any causal argument, it's important to consider whether X caused Y, or whether W caused both X and Y, or whether X and Y were both caused by independent factors, including the possibility of multiple causes.

Genuine but Insignificant Cause   There is also the causal fallacy of putting too much weight on a real but insignificant cause. In such an argument, a cause is correctly identified as such, but the argument neglects other pertinent and much more significant causes. Again, let's look at the mall franchise example. Sure the new décor may have helped, but it is a far less significant factor than the new value menu. Other more significant causes could include advertising and the business's location.

Suppressed Information

The **fallacy of exclusion** applies when there is a violation of the "principle of total evidence": a valid argument must consider all relevant information. In many cases, a precedent or supposedly analogous case is introduced as evidence, but we cannot evaluate its relevance without pertinent data. When you are developing your argument, the trick is to make sure that you don't leave out essential information or draw conclusions based on only some of the facts. Consider the entire scenario when making your case in support of your position.

Slippery Slope

This fallacy is aptly named, because it's easy to fall into the slippery trap set by the *if/then* scenario it presents. The slippery slope argues that if X happens, then Y will definitely follow. In some cases, there is a logical and definite causal relationship. But when X doesn't necessarily lead to Y, then you have slippery slope reasoning, as in the following example:

Many companies these days have "casual Fridays" when employees have the opportunity to "dress down" and come to work in polos and slacks rather than suits and ties. But casual dress leads to a casual work ethic. People feel more professional when they are dressed professionally; thus they will feel less professional when they dress casually. In addition, one day of casual attire will affect professionalism throughout the week, and employees will attempt to wear more casual attire Monday through Thursday as well. Therefore, if we implement casual Fridays, we can expect to have a less productive and less professional workforce.

There are two slippery slopes in this argument: that casual Fridays will reduce professionalism throughout the week and that casual Fridays will result in a "less productive and less professional workforce." There may indeed be a relationship between attire and professionalism, but not necessarily of the sort predicted here. In fact, casual clothes might help people feel more relaxed and comfortable at work, which may in turn *boost* productivity (not to mention employee satisfaction).

To summarize: We have reviewed the basic logical concepts as well as several specific types of fallacies that you should avoid in your essay. Familiarize yourself with these logical tools. They will equip you to quickly dismiss and avoid relying on the reasoning that will detract from your argument, saving you those precious minutes that can make the difference between a powerful, well-written essay and one that is merely acceptable.

PART THREE: THE KAPLAN FOUR-STEP METHOD FOR THE LSAT WRITING SAMPLE

As you know, you have a limited amount of time to show the law school admissions counselors that you can think logically and express yourself in clearly written English. They don't care how many syllables you can cram into a sentence or how fancy your phrases are. They care that you're making sense. Whatever you do, don't try to hide beneath a lot of hefty words and abstractions. Just make sure that everything you say is clearly written and relevant to the topic. Get in there, state your main points, back them up, and get out. Here's our four-step plan to do just that.

1. Prompt

Read the prompt carefully. Then, go back and read it again. Before you start to write, be sure you understand the prompt and the scenario it presents. As we've said before, writing off-topic is unacceptable. It suggests that you are unable to focus your ideas, or that you don't care.

2. Plan

Brainstorm to determine which alternative you will support. Think of the arguments for both courses of action and make a decision as to which one you will support. Identify your supporting examples, the number and quality of which will help you decide your position. Don't get bogged down in thinking about whether or not you agree with the position. Your argument doesn't have to express your real opinion; you only need to express a clear opinion and support it logically. Always plan your approach thoroughly before you start to write. Outline what you want to say in the introduction, in the middle paragraphs (one main idea per paragraph), and in your final paragraph. Think about how the essay as a whole will flow.

3. Produce

Use most of your time to write the essay. Start out and conclude with strong statements. Be assertive. Make transitions, link related ideas; it will help your writing flow. Start a new paragraph for each new idea and stick to your outline. Once you've started writing, you may suddenly change your mind and be tempted to alter your argument. Don't give in to that temptation! You simply won't have enough time.

4. Proofread

Save enough time after writing to read through the entire essay. Going into the LSAT, you should have a sense of the errors you are liable to make. Look out for those errors. Revise any big picture issues and correct sentence-level errors.

APPLYING THE KAPLAN FOUR-STEP METHOD

Let's use the Kaplan four-step method on the following decision prompt:

The English department at a community college must choose a new textbook for its introductory course, Composition I. Using the facts below, write an essay in which you argue for one of the following options over the other based on the following two criteria:

- *The department has a strong commitment to teaching writing skills that go beyond the basics, to prepare students to transfer to four-year programs.*

- *The department wants to increase the students' interest in writing in all areas, not just for English classes.*

During the four years that the department has used English Fundamentals, there has been a slight increase in the number of students who have won scholarships to four-year colleges after completing their degree at the community college. The text contains essays, some of them well known, from early and modern writers and is organized in sections that illustrate the various forms of the essay. Each section opens with a brief introduction explaining the basics of the essay form that is highlighted within. The essays are almost all over 10 pages and are written in a formal style. The text does not contain a specific review of grammar basics.

A new text, Writing 2.0, contains two chapters describing basic grammar and mechanics followed by several essays by contemporary authors. The pieces are typically two to three pages and cover a wide range of topics, including current events, humor, and financial and career planning. The essays range in style from informal, and even colloquial, to very formal. Each chapter contains several essays on one topic and exercises designed to aid students in

developing essays of their own. Although the grammar and mechanics chapters provide an adequate overview of basic writing skills, the text does not discuss the essay form.

1. Prompt

The scenario is an English department choosing between two textbooks. The selected textbook must support the department's commitment to teaching writing skills beyond the basics, preparing students to transfer to four-year programs, and increasing students' interest in writing.

2. Plan

Your job, as stated in the directions, is to choose one of the two textbooks and argue in support of it.

Remember, the essay isn't about showing the admissions officers that you prefer modern essays over more classic ones—or vice versa. It's about showing that you can formulate an argument and write it down. Quickly think through the pros and cons of each choice, and choose the one for which you have the most relevant and substantial support. For this topic, that process might go something like this:

Arguments for remaining with *English Fundamentals*:

- Students have been winning more scholarships.

- The text introduces them to essay forms.

- They learn how to feel comfortable reading older essays as well as modern ones.

- The formal essays demonstrate advanced writing skills, in line with the department's goal to go beyond the basics.

Arguments for switching to *Writing 2.0*:

- The chapters specifically on basic mechanics provide the students with concrete instruction.

- Contemporary authors may be more appealing to the students.

- Essays written in an informal style can demonstrate how effective writing doesn't have to be stiff.

- The practice sections provide students with defined exercises to perfect their essay writing skills.

- Range of topics show writing isn't just for English class.

Again, it doesn't really matter which side you take. Let's say that in this case you decide to argue for choosing *English Fundamentals*.

You've already begun to think out your arguments—that's why you picked the side you did in the first place. Now's the time to outline your essay. Your outline might look something like this:

Para 1:

- *EF is the better text.*

- *Students have won more scholarships*

- *Supports first goal*

- *Seeing peers win scholarships could increase enthusiasm for writing*

- *Formal style demonstrates more than just basics*

Para 2:

- *Students might be more interested in Writing 2.0 but it won't advance their skills as well as EF has and will.*

- *The informal/colloquial essays may actually harm their writing skills*

Conclusion:

EF is better b/c it is a proven text w/proven results.

4. Write Your Essay

Open your essay by stating your position. Move on to clearly identifying examples supporting your position. Then, address and refute the counterargument. In the final paragraph, restate your position.

Sample Essay

The English Fundamentals textbook is the better choice for the English department. The increased number of scholarships won by the students demonstrates that students are being well prepared for the rigors of four-year programs. The effect of the increased scholarships would influence how writing is perceived by the students; even those who do not win scholarships would recognize that being able to write well can help lead to success. This may engage the students and boost their enthusiasm and interest in writing. Although English Fundamentals relies on essays written in a formal style, which could be viewed as dry and staid by the students, the essays demonstrate mechanics, grammar and style in action. In this way, students recognize correct grammar and mechanics in actual writing.

The new textbook, Writing 2.0, with essays by contemporary writers, might seem to provide more appealing content for the students, thus adding to their interest in writing. However, the textbook relies partly on essays written in a colloquial style, which could confuse students who are still developing an understanding of writing skills. More importantly, the textbook does not cover the various forms of the essay, thus leaving a hole in the students' instruction.

In sum, English Fundamentals is the better textbook; it follows a successful formula for teaching students the basics of essay writing. This will help ensure that the English department continues to produce students who have developed an enthusiasm for writing while becoming prepared to successfully transfer to four-year colleges.

5. Proofread Your Work

Take that last couple of minutes to catch any glaring errors. Be on the lookout for spelling and punctuation errors. Pay special attention to left out words. Often, when you are rushing to write something, your mind may work more quickly than your pencil and you may find yourself leaving words out of sentences. Read each sentence slowly to make sure you've included every word.

Chapter 4 will provide you with several sample LSAT decision prompts and actual Writing Samples. Read through these and practice writing your own responses. Remember, practice makes perfect!

TIME TRIALS

Practice writing your essay under conditions that mimic those of the LSAT. Use sample decision prompts (see Chapter 4 for examples), two sheets of paper (comparable to the amount of space you'll have to write on the Writing Sample Response Sheet), and a timer set for 35 minutes. Then, write your essay. To make the situation closer to LSAT conditions, write your essay after a long day of classes or work. Better yet, write your essay after taking a timed practice LSAT exam. You will gain a sense of how well you write under pressure and how you can best prepare yourself to write a superb essay on test day.

PART FOUR: PREPARE A TEMPLATE

On test day, the Writing Sample comes at the end of the long, exhausting LSAT. And yet, you must write your essay quickly and effectively. You will be under pressure: only 35 minutes is allotted for the Writing Sample. Your best strategy is to do as much advance preparation as possible, and that means arming yourself with a template that can assist you in formulating your essay.

Of course, you will not be allowed to bring your template with you on test day. But, as you practice writing essays, you can follow the format of your template so that the organization of your essay flows quickly and easily on the big day.

Sample Template for the Writing Sample

Winner/Loser Format

Paragraph One
Objectives: Clearly identify the course of action that you have identified as the "winner" and that you will support in the essay. Provide two to three examples in support of your position.

Paragraph Two
Objective: Identify the "loser" and acknowledge and refute counterarguments.

Conclusion
Objective: Reaffirm your support of the "winner" and summarize the main points of support.

According the Criteria Format

Paragraph One
Objective: Open by stating the course of action that you will support.

Paragraph Two
Objective: Provide examples of how each course of action meets, or does not meet, the first criterion.

Paragraph Three
Objective: Provide examples of how each course of action meets, or does not meet, the second criterion.

Conclusion
Objective: Reaffirm your position and summarize the main points of support.

We've covered a lot of information in this chapter. You should feel confident that you understand the writing process involved in creating a winning LSAT Writing Sample. Through our logic skills review you know what to include in your argument and, more importantly, what to avoid. We wrapped up with an in-depth look at the Kaplan Four-Step Method for the Writing Sample and showed you how to develop templates for your essay. Now, you are ready to move on to some actual essays. The next chapter will show you several decision prompts and top-rated essays.

ANSWERS AND EXPLANATIONS

Practice 1

Paragraph 1
(1) The **advice** given to the company managers that hiring **additional** workers will result in a larger number of houses being built **contains** a fallacy of exclusion. (2) Several pieces of **vital** information are not taken into consideration in the reasoning that more workers means more houses built, **and a moment's thought** reveals that many factors other **than** merely the number of workers determines the answer to the question of how many houses will be built. (3) For example, if the construction company doesn't have enough construction equipment **or** tools to equip more **workers**, then extra workers won't help **regardless**. (4) If there aren't enough building **sites** available, **enough raw materials**, or sufficient infrastructure to support additional workers, then hiring more workers might well **be** just a waste of money. (5) The whole question of diminishing returns **in increasing staff size** is not considered by this line of reasoning at all.

(1) *Advice* is the noun; *advise* is a verb.
More additional is an example of pleonasm (redundancy).
Advice is the singular subject of the sentence, so it takes the singular verb form, *contains*.

(2) *Extremely vital* is redundant.
This sentence is a run-on—two independent clauses joined by a comma with no conjunction. Fix it by either adding a conjunction or making it into two sentences (or possibly by swapping the comma for a semicolon).
Moment's is possessive here, so it takes an apostrophe.
Reasoning is repetitive with the preceding clause, so swap it out for another term such as *thought*.
The sentence compares the number of workers with the other factors, so the comparative *than* is required.
The final question is embedded, so it takes a period rather than a question mark.

(3) Omit the slash as a substitute for the conjunction *or* in AWA essays.
Workers is a simple plural here, so no apostrophe is necessary.
Always use *regardless* rather than *irregardless*.

(4) The sentence here refers to building locations (*sites*), not things seen (*sights*).
The middle term in this series violates parallelism in the original, creating confusion.
The future conditional subjunctive here takes the verb *be* rather than *been*.

(5) The phrase *in increasing staff size* modifies the question of diminishing returns, so put the modifier next to the thing it modifies in order to avoid confusion.

Paragraph 2
(1) While the **school board's** argument that eating breakfast **in the school breakfast program** is related to a reduction of absenteeism may be convincing, (2) **the** conclusion that forcing more students to eat breakfast on the school program will cause a **decrease** in absences is unwarranted.
(3) The **statistics** show a **correspondence** that is far from clear enough to assume causation.
(4) The attendance of students at the school-sponsored breakfast program and at subsequent

classes **might** both result from a third, unexamined cause that creates the observed **effect**. (5) For example, students who eat school breakfasts **every day** might just happen to be the ones who go to bed early [no comma] and therefore are up in time for both the breakfast and for classes. (6) Or **perhaps** the students with better attendance experience a different kind of parent supervision that contributes to both **their** better diet and their improved attendance.

(1) *School board* is a common noun, so no capitals. If it were the name of a specific school board, for example the Shelby County School Board, then it would be capitalized.
In the school breakfast program modifies *eating breakfast*, so it should go closer to what it modifies in order to avoid confusion about what exactly is in the program.
This sentence is a fragment because of the subordinate *while* at the beginning. One easy way to fix this problem is to join it to the next sentence by changing the period to a comma and eliminating the capital letter at the beginning of the next sentence as shown.

(2) *Decreasing drop* is redundant.

(3) *Statistics* is a simple plural, not a possessive, so no apostrophe is needed.
Correspondence is misspelled.

(4) *Maybe* is a lowbrow qualifier; prefer *might* or *perhaps*.
Effect is the noun that describes an influence or outcome. The noun *affect* is psychological jargon for "emotion."

(5) The word *everyday* means "ordinary." The phrase *every day* means "happening on each day." The phrase that follows the conjunction *and* is not an independent clause (it shares its subject with the clause before the conjunction) so the comma is omitted in this case.

(6) *Maybe* is a lowbrow qualifier; prefer *might* or *perhaps*.
Keep the perspective consistent, *and* try to avoid the use of *one* as a pronoun.

Paragraph 3
(1) In surveying their customers and **finding** that **most** prefer games with lifelike graphics, the computer game company has correctly identified a cause for an increase in the popularity of particular game types. (2) From the evidence presented, it seems **reasonable** that certain customers buy the more lifelike games in preference to games with **inferior** graphics. (3) However, the conclusion that game sales will rise as **a result** of this action neglects to take into account the evidence (4) that the more lifelike games require the latest computer hardware. (5) The argument presents no evidence that the target audience is undergoing a transition to this more advanced, **and more expensive,** type of computer platform. (6) **On the contrary,** common sense seems to suggest that, since the target audience tends to be young, their earning power would not allow them to acquire the equipment necessary to **accommodate** the games in question, and thus **the change in emphasis** would not necessarily result in increased sales of those games. (7) If the company **were** to invest in **development** of these games, **it** might waste money in the end.

(1) The company has been *surveying* and *finding*. Changing the verb form to *found* in the original version violates parallelism and creates confusion.
It's not clear in the original version who *they* refers to: it could be the customers or the company. Changing the pronoun clarifies that it is the customers who prefer lifelike games.

(2) *Okay* is a lowbrow modifier; *reasonable* is more appropriate.
The comma after the introductory clause *From the evidence presented* is technically optional, but probably helps prevent possible confusion in this case.
Might maybe is too tentative.
Worse is too lowbrow to be consistent with the tone of the rest of the paragraph; prefer *inferior*.

(3) *End result* is redundant.

(4) This sentence is a fragment. One easy way to fix the problem is to join this sentence to the previous one. Since it is a restrictive clause (beginning with *that*) it doesn't need a comma or conjunction—just remove the period and the initial capital letter.
New and *latest* together are redundant.

(5) Omit the wordy filler phrase *to show the fact that*
And more expensive is a parenthetic phrase, so it should be set off by commas.

(6) Add a comma after the introductory phrase *On the contrary*.
Omit the qualifier *perhaps* in this case because, in combination with the verb *suggests*, it comes across as overly tentative.
Accommodate is misspelled in the original.
The referent of the pronoun *it* is unclear in the original version. Specify what *it* is with a specific phrase such as *the change in emphasis* as shown.

(7) The subjunctive conditional in this sentence takes the *were* form of the verb.
Development is misspelled in the original.

Practice 2

1. Competition and cooperation are not mutually exclusive: think of team sports or corporate business ventures.

2. Educational systems have many goals; instilling values and providing job training are both important. Other goals include recreation, fitness training, and public service.

3. Government spending is more complicated than a choice between the arts and social services: a way can be found to afford both. Or, what about art institutions such as museums, artists' colonies, and grant programs that provide social services (employment, daycare, support) and advance the arts at the same time?

4. It might show good work ethics to quit a job that you're not enthusiastic about, but it is a false dilemma. Other alternatives include staying at your job but not working hard, or working hard and then quitting anyway.

5. Alternatives to this false dilemma include the possibility that some supporters of the bill understood it and thought that it would be good for America anyway, or that they didn't understand it but weren't thinking about the good of America at all—among others.

6. …or maybe the chess champion will win and feel great anyway, or he'll lose and be impressed, pleased, or relieved.

Practice 3

1. Any of the many cases where the rights of individuals come into conflict with each other is a good exception to this generalization. For example, a restaurant owner's right to try and make a profit doesn't supersede his/her customer's right to healthy food: that's why we have health department regulations.

2. There are many factors that contribute to commercial success: efficiency and quality are obviously important, for instance. Originality may be useful, but imitation can certainly be profitable.

3. There are many "vital" qualities for a leader. For example the ability to get other people to follow must be just as important as the ability to make decisions.

4. This generalization suggests that the only way to understand the difficulties that face public school teachers is to be one. That's not necessarily true: the difficulties can be understood by observation or study, or a person could be a teacher and still not think that it was difficult.

5. The generalization here lies in connecting "practical research" (whatever that is) with enjoyable life. A lot of technologies that make life more enjoyable—for example the Graphite materials used in different kinds of sporting equipment—comes from general or abstract research.

6. This statement contains a false dilemma (style and substance are not mutually exclusive) but it also contains an overstated generalization in the assertion that "everyone thinks" style is more important. Any example of a person or group that values substance over style is a good example for attacking this generalization.

Practice 4

Conclusion: Brockhoff should become the athletic director of the district.
Premises:

- Mr. Brockhoff began as the head coach five years ago.

- In the last five years, the team has won three championships.

- In the last five years, the quality of athletic facilities has improved.

As with all inductive arguments, the conclusion here is invalid. The premises show that Mr. Brockhoff's tenure coincides with an improvement in the athletics program of the school, so you can infer a relationship. But there's not necessarily a relationship: it might just be a coincidence, or there may be a confusion between causes and effects here. For example, an improvement in the athletic equipment may have caused the championships without any contribution from the coach. Furthermore, there's no evidence to suggest that Mr. Brockhoff's ability as a football coach necessarily makes him a good general director. It's impossible to know whether the conclusion is true or not, but it isn't necessarily false either.

Practice 5

In this situation, the conclusion implicitly bears on *all people of all ages*. Yet the study group is extremely limited. Any of the distinguishing characteristics of the sample group (that the subjects were women, that they were Belgian, that they were over eighty years old, that they lived in assisted care, and that they exercised) could have introduced factors that do not apply to the population as a whole.

Practice 6

In this instance, the differences in size and location between the size and location of the two restaurants invalidate any inference you could make about the impact of table service on their relative popularity.

Chapter 4: **LSAT Prompts and Sample Essays**

This chapter contains 25 sample prompts for the Issue task and 25 sample prompts for the Argument task. For your convenience, there are three pages of write-on lines. The page after the prompt is for you to plan your essay, the following two pages are for you to write the essay.

PROMPT #1

Berthe Collison is considering two different job offers for a position in her field of sales. Keeping the following considerations in mind, write an argument supporting one of the two job offers described.

- Berthe needs to make at least $65,000 per year in order for her to cover her bills and debts, while allowing her to save up money for a down payment on a house.

- Berthe and her husband have two small children.

One job offer is as a regional sales position in the lucrative field of pharmaceuticals. The base salary is $55,000 with the opportunity to earn up to a $20,000 end-of-year bonus, depending on her ability to meet sales quotas. The job offers full medical but not dental benefits. The work Berthe would do is not office-based, so Berthe could make her own schedule. She will be given a company car but will have to pay for gas. Because the job covers the entire region of the southwestern United States, she will be required to travel out of state a minimum of two days per week. The job comes with 15 paid vacation days per year.

The other job offer is as a sales manager for a local company with a solid history of success and job security. Because Berthe would only be managing a team of sales representatives, she is not entitled to any sales commissions, and her salary would be $62,000 per year. The company's offices are located about 10 minutes from her house. Berthe would have her own office and a private parking space. She would receive medical and dental coverage but would have to pay a $200 per month co-pay. This position offers 20 vacation days per year and the office hours are 8 A.M. to 3 P.M.

PROMPT #1 SAMPLE ESSAY

Berthe should choose the job as sales manager of a local company.

As the mother of two small children, Berthe would benefit from being home and not having the stress of weekly travel out of state. The sales manager job provides an easy commute with an office that is within minutes of her home. Not only will Berthe be near her kids if they need her, she will have the space that she needs to work outside of the home, as well as the convenience of free parking. The set work hours for the job are ideal for a working mother because they begin and end around the time that children are in and out of school.

The regional sales position job is one that would provide financially for Berthe but most likely will be very stressful physically and mentally. The required weekly travel, gas payments and pressure to make sales quotas to meet her $65,000 yearly goal may cause strain to her daily activities outside of the workplace. In addition, the lack of dental benefits will impact her out-of-pocket expenses in order to cover her whole family.

The sales manager position is more convenient for Berthe's lifestyle. It is a secure job that provides full medical and dental benefits. Although the out-of-pocket benefit co-pays are high, her consistent salary, short commute, and free parking make up for it.

While there is opportunity for growth and success with both job positions, the sales manager job fits Berthe's life better professionally and personally.

PROMPT #2

The small business Charlie's Chocolate Dipped Strawberries has requested proposals from two fresh produce suppliers to determine which vendor will be the company's exclusive supplier of strawberries for use in their final product. Keeping the following considerations in mind, write an argument supporting which one of the suppliers Charlie's should sign a contract with.

- In order to ensure the customer the freshest final product, the strawberries need to be at the factory for dipping within nine hours of harvesting.

- Charlie's requires a reliable and fresh supply of strawberries at the lowest price, regardless of the season. The maximum Charlie's can pay is $0.55 a pound, as long as delivery fees are included.

Freshen Farms is a small, family-owned farm that produces strawberries year round. In the regular harvest season, the berries are grown outside, and cost $0.40 a pound. In off-season months, berries are grown in controlled environments such as greenhouses, and the price goes up to $0.60. The family has run the farm for three generations, and 10 members of the family participate in everyday operations. The strawberries are inspected for color, size, and shape when harvested, and again when they are carefully packaged by hand into crates designed to cause minimal damage. Freshen Farms is a three-hour drive from the factory. The cost of delivery is not included in the price of the berries and isn't fixed, due to rising gas prices and the cost of maintaining the one delivery truck that Freshen owns.

Best Berries is a large, corporately owned berry farm. They produce strawberries, blueberries, raspberries, and boysenberries. All berries are grown in controlled environments, and although picking is done by hand, machines separate berries by size and package the produce in recyclable containers. The farm is an approximately eight-hour drive from Charlie's. It offers a fixed price of $0.65 a pound that is inclusive of delivery costs. In addition, if Charlie's demand for strawberries increases, Best Berries can meet an increased demand up to 300 percent with no problem.

_____

_____

_____

_____

_____

_____

_____

_____

_____

_____

_____

_____

_____

_____

_____

_____

_____

_____

_____

_____

_____

_____

_____

_____

_____

_____

_____

_____

_____

_____

_____

_____

_____

_____

_____

_____

_____

_____

_____

_____

_____

_____

_____

_____

_____

_____

_____

_____

_____

_____

_____

_____

_____

_____

_____

_____

_____

_____

_____

_____

_____

_____

_____

_____

_____

_____

PROMPT #2 SAMPLE ESSAY

Charlie's Chocolate Dipped Strawberries should choose Freshen Farms as their exclusive strawberry vendor.

Freshen Farms meets Charlie's criteria all around. Although they are slightly higher in price in the off season months, their strawberries are cared for personally, and hand picked. As a family owned business, Charlie's can rest assured that they are paying for a strawberry that is well maintained from plantation to packaging.

The Best Berries product does have a few advantages. Although the price per pound for Best Berries strawberries is five cents more than Charlie's would like to pay, that price includes delivery. Best Berries can also guarantee that it can meet increased demand, should Charlie's business take off. However, Charlie's requires that the strawberries be ready for dipping no more than nine hours from the time of harvest. The eight-hour distance that separates Charlie's from Best Berries doesn't leave Charlie's with a lot of time to complete the dipping. In addition, the strawberries at Best Berries are not inspected for the quality of color or shape. Also, the packaging used by Best Berries, while recyclable, is not maximized to protect the strawberries from bruising during travel. Therefore, Charlie's would have to make sacrifices in quality and efficiency to use the Best Berries product.

With Freshen Farms, Charlie's is taking the chance on spending a little more on delivery with the ever increasing gas prices. But Charlie's would be able to maintain its quality standards, meaning the customer will be happy with the quality of the final product, and as a result would buy more and keep coming back.

Freshen Farms and Best Berries are two companies that produce quality fruit, but for Charlie's specific business needs, Freshen Farms is the better fit.

PROMPT #3

Optimum Health, a holistic care company, is looking for the best way to market their newest vitamin supplement, Never Need a Sick Day, which is meant to promote health and prevent missed work because of the common cold. Keeping the following considerations in mind, write an argument supporting which one of the following marketing campaigns Optimum Health should use.

- The primary target audience is single, paid by the hour, working people who are most affected by missing work, but Optimum Health also aims to reach parents of children who are often absent from school due to illness.

- Although Optimum Health products are found in many stores, 50 percent of its sales come from its website.

The first marketing campaign is designed as a blanket campaign. The money spent by Optimum Health will be evenly distributed between print advertisements in national magazines and newsletters, online banner ads, and radio commercials in the top three cities in which Optimum Health sells the most products. The firm that will handle this campaign has been successful with other health products, but it will be the first time that it is representing Optimum Health. The budget for this campaign is $100,000 and is expected to increase net profit by about 2 percent.

The second marketing campaign is a targeted campaign. Online customers at Optimum Health's website were asked various buying preferences and demographic details. Based on this information collected, the campaign is focusing on web advertising only. This will include banner advertisements on various websites, including partner websites related to healthy living and cooking. Optimum Health will also offer an incentive program to current website visitors to provide the names of potential customers in order to receive 40 percent off their next purchase. This campaign is expected to cost $50,000.

_____

_____

_____

_____

_____

_____

_____

_____

_____

_____

_____

_____

_____

_____

_____

_____

_____

_____

_____

_____

_____

_____

PROMPT #3 SAMPLE ESSAY

Optimum Health should choose the second online marketing campaign to advertise their products.

The target audiences for Optimum Health products are young professionals and young parents. This demographic spends the majority of their time on the Internet whether it is at work or at home. They check their news online, buy online, and send messages online. Advertising Optimum Health products on various websites that the target audience may visit will increase profit and popularity for the company. With 50 percent of the sales already coming from its website alone, it only makes sense to continue advertising online.

The first blanketing campaign is unique because it offers many venues for advertising. This will get Optimum Health's name out there in many forms. Unfortunately, this advertising firm does not know Optimum Health products, or what their customers want. It is an overpriced campaign that will bring in a small net profit. In the end it may not even out with what Optimum Health is paying them up front to get their name out there.

The second marketing campaign has done their research. They know what the customers of Optimum Health prefer and need. Providing them with a substantial discount incentive for bringing in more business is a smart move that will multiply with the increase of customers.

Optimum Health will pay less for the second marketing campaign and have a net profit way over 2 percent due to smart advertising, knowing the customers, and making them happy. Hands down, they are the smart choice.

PROMPT #4

The city of Descanso is looking to construct a brand new community center for after-school programs, town hall meetings, and private functions such as weddings. They have narrowed their design choices down to plans from two architectural firms, Gutierrez Design Group and Krantz & Associates. Keeping the following considerations in mind, write an argument supporting which one of the following building plans the city should proceed with.

- The population of Descanso is expected to grow rapidly in the next five years.

- The anticipated, but not yet finalized, budget for this project is $1.2 million.

The design by Krantz & Associates is modest in scale. The building itself would consist of a small administrative office, one large hall, and a medium-size kitchen. The hall would be installed with retractable walls to divide the space into different configurations, depending on the intended use. This design also includes a playground and a field that can be used for various purposes, including football, soccer, or baseball games and track and field events. The building would have total occupancy of 350, and would cost approximately $570,000 to complete.

The design by the Gutierrez Design Group has a large open-plan hall that can accommodate 150 occupants, two smaller classroom-style rooms, a large conference room, and a large kitchen. The design also incorporates an entrance that can be used as a display area. For example, at the community center's opening, the entrance would be decorated with photographs from the last 100 years of the town's history. There is no outdoor space planned, but there will be an additional room dedicated solely to afterschool programs. The total occupancy of this building is 550 and the proposed cost is $1.3 million.

PROMPT #4 SAMPLE ESSAY

The city of Descanso should choose the community center design by the Gutierrez Design Group.

One of the city's criteria is to plan for rapid population growth in the next five years. In fact, the need for more space will seem to arrive even sooner, considering the 6 to 12 months it will take to build the center. The total occupancy of the Krantz & Associates building is only 350, while the Gutierrez building would hold up to 550. Moreover, the Krantz design is described as "modest in scale" and is not flexible enough in its use of space to accommodate growth. For example, although the Krantz design does have retractable walls in its large hall, the Gutierrez plan has more rooms and of varied function. While the Krantz plan does include a small administrative office—and the Gutierrez plan does not—it is reasonable that a reception desk and phone could be placed in the entrance area of the Gutierrez design.

Furthermore, the Gutierrez entrance offers additional space for community displays and exhibits, a ticket booth, after-school child pickup, and field trip assembly. Although the Krantz plan includes a playground and a field, both rely upon good weather, and sports are not mentioned in the city's criteria. Regardless, after-school indoor sports and games could be played in the large Gutierrez hall. The fact that the Gutierrez Group includes a dedicated after-school room and two classrooms allows for population growth as well as multi-use space for tutoring and homework, arts and crafts, games, a computer lab, and adult education classes. Finally, the large kitchen in the Gutierrez design works for all sizes of weddings, dinners, board meetings, and after-school snacking.

While the Krantz plan comes in at $570,000, it does not maximize the finances available. Additionally, the savings is not worth the loss of flexible and expandable space that is offered by the slightly more expensive Gutierrez alternative. Thus, for its expected growth and multi-use needs, the city of Descanso should choose the Gutierrez Design Group as their architectural firm.

PROMPT #5

The Clark family lives in the desert of Arizona. To lower their utility bills and to help the environment, the Clarks would like to convert their home's heating and electricity to an alternative energy source. Their current cost of heating and electricity is $3,500. They have two alternative energy plans. Keeping the following considerations in mind, write an argument supporting which one of the following forms of alternative energy they should pursue.

- The Clarks have $7,000 in savings dedicated to setting up their alternative energy source.

- They are planning to move out of Arizona in about 10 years.

The first alternative energy source the Clarks are considering is solar power. There are 320 days of sun where they live. Solar panels can provide both heating for water and electricity to power their home, and in this case, their bill will be reduced by 60 percent. Installing a solar panel occurs in three phases: consultation for the design, installation (cost: $500 per square meter), and maintenance (cost: a flat fee of $1,000 annually for the first 2 years, and $2,000 for years 3 to 10). The solar company has estimated that the Clarks will need to install at least 16 square meters of panels but installation can be done in a single day.

The second alternative energy source the Clarks are considering is geothermal power. Government surveys have estimated that the well will have to be drilled at least 100 feet deep on their property and the drilling will take about 5 to 7 business days. Before they can take advantage of geothermal energy, their specific property will have to be surveyed, the ground drilled, and the power and heat generator installed. The cost for these steps can run from $10,000 to $12,000, but the use of geothermal energy will essentially eliminate monthly heat and electricity utility bills. Every six months, the site will require a routine inspection at a cost of $200.

_____

_____

_____

_____

_____

_____

_____

_____

_____

_____

_____

_____

_____

_____

_____

_____

_____

_____

_____

_____

_____

_____

_____

_____

_____

_____

_____

_____

_____

_____

_____

_____

_____

_____

_____

_____

_____

_____

_____

_____

_____

_____

_____

PROMPT #5 SAMPLE ESSAY

The Clark family should pursue the geothermal power alternative in converting their home's energy source.

Both systems—geothermal and solar—are green, renewable energy sources that improve the environment. Neither system can be taken with them when they move in 10 years. The geothermal choice, however, is more financially sound than the solar choice in this case.

During the 10 years the Clarks are considering staying in this Arizona home, the geothermal alternative energy source costs less in maintenance and gains more in utility savings. The solar choice reduces the Clarks' utility bill by only 60%, saving them about $2,100 a year. With the geothermal alternative, the Clarks will save money immediately, going from about $292 a month to $0.

Additionally, the maintenance of the solar alternative over ten years will be about $18,000 next to the projected $4,000 of the geothermal choice. Adding in installation costs, the solar alternative would cost the Clarks about $26,000 to install ($8,000 for 16 square meters and $18,000 to maintain) over 10 years and save them about $21,000 in bills. This is far less attractive than the geothermal choice, which will cost about $14,000–$16,000 and save about $35,000. Although the geothermal system costs more than the Clarks' budgeted $7,000, just the energy bill savings of $3,500 per year, minus the $400 inspection costs, would pay back a loan of $5,000 in a very short amount of time.

In addition, where the Clarks live there is an annual average of 320 days of sun. The fact that geothermal power relies on renewable power harnessed underground means that it is not dependant upon the weather, as solar power is. Also, the geothermal alternative has stronger selling points if the Clarks sell their house in 10 years; there are no heating and electrical bills, and only $400 inspection costs per year.

The geothermal energy plan will save the Clarks more money in the long term and make the house more attractive to buyers in 10 years.

PROMPT #6

Recent college graduates and newlyweds Chris and Jikja Jansen are looking to purchase a new car so that Chris can commute 25 miles to and from work on weekdays, and that Jikja, who works from home, can run errands and do shopping in the evenings and on weekends. Keeping the following considerations in mind, write an argument supporting one of the two car options described.

- The Jansens have $3,500 in savings and would need to keep any payments down to only about $150 a month.

- Chris and Jikja plan on starting a family in about a year.

Option 1 is a used, two-door, compact convertible with automatic transmission. It has many upgraded features such as power locks, power windows, CD player, and leather upholstering. They do not know the previous owners, but no serious problems appeared on the CARFAX vehicle history report they got from the dealer. The car gets a limited four-year warranty from the dealership and was recently equipped with brand new tires. Also, the Jansens have taken the car on two separate test drives, and it seems to be in good condition. It has 87,000 miles on it and gets average gas mileage. There is a theft prevention device installed, and the resale value of this car remains steady. It costs $4,000.

Option 2 is a brand new, four-door sedan with manual transmission. To get the lowest price, they are looking to buy the standard model, which does not have additional features such as power locks or power windows. It comes with a four-year or 100,000 mile warranty, has the highest safety rating available on a new car, and gets excellent gas mileage. The cost of this vehicle is $15,700. The Jansens would have to lease the car from the dealership; it's a $3,000 down payment, and then $169 a month for three years.

_____

_____

_____

_____

_____

_____

_____

_____

_____

_____

_____

_____

_____

_____

_____

_____

_____

_____

_____

_____

_____

_____

_____

_____

_____

_____

_____

_____

_____

_____

_____

_____

_____

_____

_____

_____

_____

_____

_____

_____

_____

_____

_____

_____

PROMPT #6 SAMPLE ESSAY

The Jansens should choose Option 2—to lease the brand-new sedan.

The couple's first consideration is that they are newlyweds with only $3,500 in savings. The Option 1 car has a theft prevention device, which can lower insurance premiums, a steady resale value, and a cost of $4,000, which is only slightly more than our young couple has saved. However, it gets only average gas mileage. And although it appears to be in good condition, it's used and has only a limited warranty, which means that the Jansens would have to pay out-of-pocket if unexpected problems arise.

If they lease the new car of Option 2, the Jansens will have enough for the down payment of $3,000 and the first month's lease. Although the monthly lease payments are about $20 more than the couple has budgeted for monthly payments, they will have a new car with a full warranty that gets excellent gas mileage.

Chris and Jikja's second consideration is their plan to start a family. Option 2 provides more room for all the equipment that's required for driving with an infant in a car. Moreover, the sedan has an excellent safety rating, which provides the young couple with peace of mind. While Option 2 car has no power locks, standard-model car locks can be manually set so as not to be manipulated by little children's hands.

The Option 2 sedan is larger, has a more extensive warranty, and is within financial reach, making it the best choice for the Jansens.

PROMPT #7

Jillian and Darren Greene have just moved into a rented home in Portland, Oregon. Because they now have a small yard, they would like to adopt a dog from the local shelter. They have narrowed their choices to two dogs. Keeping the following considerations in mind, write an argument supporting which breed of dog they should adopt.

- The Greenes have two small children, so they want a dog that is small and friendly. They have an 18-month-old boy, Charles, and a 4-year-old girl, Abby, who has asthma problems.

- In addition to the costs of owning a pet, dogs weighing over 40 pounds add $50 extra to the monthly rent.

One dog is a 1-year-old shiba inu. These small dogs never weigh more than 25 pounds. They require some training and behavior conditioning to mellow out their naturally fiery temperaments, but once that is done, they are good with adults, and okay with children as long as they are not provoked. They do not require any special diets, are generally healthy animals, and live about 12 to 15 years. This breed sheds its fur a great deal in warm weather (75 degrees Fahrenheit and up).

The other dog the Greenes are considering adopting is a standard poodle, which is a larger dog that can weigh up to 70 pounds. One distinguishing feature is that they have hair, not fur, so they are a great choice for people who have pet fur allergies, but their hair does require regular grooming, which can be costly if done professionally. Poodles are known for being easily trainable, intelligent, and easy going; they are ideal for houses with children. The breed has a reputation for being susceptible to a lot of health issues, some very serious, and an average life span of about 11 to 12 years.

PROMPT #7 SAMPLE ESSAY

The Greene family should adopt the standard poodle from the local shelter.

The poodle has two significant traits that fit in with this family's first consideration. Both issues are significant because they relate to the vital health and safety of the family. The shiba inu has fur and sheds it a lot in warm weather, which Portland experiences at least 5 months of the year. By contrast, the poodle has hair—not fur—which would not exacerbate young Abby's asthma, or bother any family member or guest with pet fur allergies. Asthma has the potential to be a very serious condition that can worsen with age, so this health issue is likely of premier importance to the Greenes.

Second, the shiba inu breed requires "behavioral conditioning to mellow out their natural fiery temperaments" and even with this, the shiba inus only get along with children as long as they are not provoked. The Greene children are both under 5 years old and, therefore, very likely to play rough. The Greenes shouldn't choose a dog that might scare or bite Charles, Abby, or one of their friends. On the other hand, the standard poodle breed is very trainable and easy-going—ideal for a family with very young children.

Financial issues are the Greenes' second consideration. If the poodle grows to be more than 40 pounds, Darren and Jillian will need to put aside savings for that eventuality or negotiate with their landlord. In terms of health problems or other expenses, this is an unknown that is always a risk when you adopt a pet, especially from a shelter. And while the poodle needs regular grooming, this can be managed if the Greenes learn how to groom the dog themselves.

Although both breeds have advantages and disadvantages for the Greenes, they should choose the standard poodle, due mostly to health and safety issues for their children.

PROMPT #8

The Munk College Graduation Celebration committee is deciding where to hold an important dinner event following the commencement ceremony on campus to honor distinguished alumni and this year's graduates. Because this is the centennial year of the school, the celebration will serve the dual purpose of also recognizing the school's history. Keeping the following considerations in mind, write an argument supporting one of the two locations described.

- The committee has a budget of $100,000 for an anticipated guest list of 1,500.

- There must be space to display the school's large memorabilia collection.

The first location of choice for the event is the local armory. It is a beautiful historic building that is within walking distance of the campus, approximately 10 minutes. It also has a connection to the college in that it is dedicated to the school's founder, and there are banners draped around the hall that show Munk's school colors. Because the armory is in the middle of downtown, there is only on-site free parking for about 200 cars. However, the parking lots of the campus could be used. There is also a parking garage nearby that charges $10 an hour. The armory is just one open-plan hall, and its occupancy is 1,200. Although the building has its original décor, the kitchen facilities were renovated in the 1990s for catering events. The price for a catered event is $60 per person, which includes a kitchen staff and waiters. Tables and chairs can be rented for $15,000. The cost of decorating the room (flowers, table cloths, chair covers, and labor) will be approximately $3,500, and the DJ/MC costs $2,000, bringing the grand total to a minimum of $110,500.

The Waverly Plaza is a new hotel that just opened up outside of the town where Munk College is located. It is a 20-minute drive from the campus. The Grand Ballroom at the hotel, which holds 1,700 guests for a seated dinner, is available for that evening. It has a removable dance floor and an elegant entry hall. All facilities and equipment are top of the line. The price is $80 per person, which includes a kitchen staff and waiters. There is ample parking available, but Munk College will have to use the hotel's valet parking service, which costs $10,000. Decorating costs for the room (flowers, tablecloths, chair covers, and labor) will be approximately $8,000, and the DJ/MC costs $2,000, bringing the grand total to a minimum of $140,000.

PROMPT #8 SAMPLE ESSAY

The Munk College Graduation Celebration committee should hold the dinner event at the local armory.

As a historical building dedicated to Munk College's founder and decorated with banners displaying Munk's school colors, the armory will provide a distinctive backdrop for the celebratory dinner. The committee can use the armory's ambiance as a foundation for its decoration plans, which will support its goal of recognizing the school's history in its centennial year. In order to display the college's memorabilia collection—one of the committee's main goals for the event—Munk College will have to create extra space within the hall. They will also have to scale down the guest list to accommodate the 1,200 occupancy limit. Nevertheless, the cost of holding the event at the local armory is $110,500, which is very close the committee's budget of $100,000.

The Waverly Plaza does have a few advantages over the local armory. Whereas the local armory has only limited on-site parking, the Waverly Plaza has sufficient on-site parking, and it will be free-of-charge for the guests. In addition, the ballroom has sample space for the estimated 1,500 guests estimated to attend, and the elegant entry hall is a convenient place to display the school's large memorabilia collection. However, the event would cost approximately $140,000, which is significantly more than the committee has in their budget.

In sum, while each location has its benefits, with its historical ties to the college and the estimated lower overall costs, the local armory is the better location for the Munk College Graduation Celebration dinner.

PROMPT #9

Jeremy Jordan is planning his schedule for his last semester of college. Because he has already met the requirements for his major, he can choose one course to take for his own interest. Keeping the following considerations in mind, write an argument supporting which one of the two courses Jeremy should register for.

- Jeremy must maintain his high grade point average.

- Jeremy wants to be a sports therapist—a physical therapist with a concentration in sports medicine.

Option 1 is a course on the History of American Sports. This course covers the history and details of major American sports such as basketball, football, baseball, and tennis. The coursework requires a lot of reading and the majority of the grade is dependent on a research paper that each student must write about a particular sport. The class meets once per week. The professor is engaging in class, and while he does have official office hours, his door is always open. He has been known to write wonderful letters of reference for those students who have put in hard work and earned good grades in this course.

Option 2 is Advanced Biology. Jeremy already took a biology course and did well. The renowned professor who teaches this upper-level course is known for pushing his students and also for being a very strict grader. This course will require lab time that will work with Jeremy's school schedule, but will require him to sacrifice more of his free time throughout the week. Coursework includes 2 exams and many quizzes and lab reports. There is an extra lab fee associated with registering for this course. The jobs Jeremy has started to research do require a strong science background.

PROMPT #9 SAMPLE ESSAY

Jeremy Jordan should register for the Advanced Biology course in his last semester.

One of Jeremy's goals for his last semester is to maintain his high grade point average. While the Advanced Biology course may appear to be more difficult and demanding than the History of American Sports, Jeremy has already proven that he has the potential to achieve a high grade by doing well in an earlier biology course. This foundation will allow him to respond favorably to being pushed by the demanding Advance Biology professor. In addition, the course will be graded based on two exams, many quizzes and lab reports. This structure will enable Jeremy to receive feedback on his work throughout the semester. This will help him to gauge how well he is doing and make any necessary changes to ensure a high grade. In contrast, the History of American Sports grade depends on one major research paper. There is significant risk involved in relying on only one paper for a grade. Should Jeremy not do well on the paper, he would not have an opportunity to improve his grade for the course, which would have a negative impact on his overall grade point average.

The Advanced Biology course would also better support Jeremy's interest in becoming a sports therapist. Jeremy has found that the jobs he is researching require him to have a strong science background. The Advanced Biology course, with its rigorous lab work, would bolster Jeremy's knowledge and skills. When applying for sports therapist jobs, Jeremy could highlight his biology coursework to increase his appeal to potential employers. In the History of American Sports course, on the other hand, Jeremy would develop a greater understanding of the details of the major sports. However, his research would focus primarily on one sport, which would have only a limited benefit for his future career goals.

Thus, the Advance Biology course is the better choice for Jeremy's last semester because it is more likely to ensure his high grade point average and help achieve his goal of becoming a sports therapist.

PROMPT #10

Medical Miracles is a seasonally published magazine featuring breakthrough products that prevent or treat some of the most ubiquitous medical maladies. The magazine's publishers are deciding on a cover story for an upcoming issue. Keeping the following considerations in mind, write an argument supporting one of the two cover stories described.

- This story will be featured in the summer issue of Medical Miracles.

- Medical Miracles has a reputation for featuring only the most groundbreaking new treatments.

The first cover story features Lanitor, which is designed to aid in weight loss. Lanitor will be available by prescription only, but is shown to increase weight loss by 5 percent when combined with diet and exercise. The makers of Lanitor also produce Govun, a medicine used in the treatment of a particular eye disease. Govun has been on the market for several years for a different ailment, but a recent study showed that Govun has excellent success rates for slowing this eye disease's progress. Govun is not available over the counter and there are no generic brand alternatives.

The second cover story features a new lotion. When used properly and consistently, this product can protect the skin from 100 percent of harmful UV rays (both UVa and UVb), which are known to cause skin cancer. It combines the highest SPF available with a powerful agent that can reverse the tell-tale signs of skin damage and premature skin aging in just six weeks. This lotion is easily applied, thoroughly absorbed, and waterproof. People with sensitive skin have suffered rashes from using this lotion. It is also not recommended for children under the age of 5. It offers the best sun protection available on the market and is competitively priced with other sun protection lotions.

PROMPT #10 SAMPLE ESSAY

Medical Miracles should feature the new sun protection lotion as its cover story for the summer issue.

The lotion provides significant protection against harmful UV rays, making it a timely topic for the summer magazine. Although people do use sun protection lotion throughout the year, they are more likely to consider their sun protection options during summer when they are exposed to the sun's rays. Thus, the cover story on the new lotion would be attractive to the magazine's readership. A cover story on Lanitor would be more appropriate for another time of the year. Although people are often concerned with their weight during the summer, they are more likely to be interested in losing weight before summer arrives. Therefore, a cover story on Lanitor would be a season too late; it would not be as timely as one on the new lotion.

Featuring the new lotion as the cover story also supports Medical Miracles' record of highlighting groundbreaking new products. The new lotion is truly innovative: it offers the best sun protection available on the market, with the highest SPF available, and contains ingredients that reverse signs of skin damage and premature skin aging. The ability of the lotion to protect the skin from 100 percent of UVa and UVb rays, however, is the most revolutionary feature of the product. Since the UV rays are known to cause skin cancer, by protecting against them 100 percent, the new lotion has the potential to significantly reduce skin cancer incidents. Moreover, the lotion is competitively priced with other sun protection lotions on the market. This is an additional benefit of the product because consumers will not have to pay a premium to receive the best sun protection available. The combination of the lotion's groundbreaking features and competitive price make it a compelling product to feature on the cover of the summer issue of Medical Miracles.

Lanitor also treats a common malady, but in a much more conservative fashion than the new lotion. Whereas the new lotion protects against 100 percent of the UV rays that cause skin cancer, Lanitor helps increase weight loss by five percent when combined with diet and exercise.

This is a much more ordinary effect of weight loss aids. Thus, Lanitor would not provide Medical Miracles with the type of groundbreaking cover story for which it has a reputation for featuring.

As an innovative new treatment that is particularly relevant in the summer season, the new lotion is the more appropriate choice for the Medical Miracles summer issue cover story.

PART TWO

Law School Admissions

Chapter 5: **Writing an Effective Law School Admission Essay**

There are thousands of theories on what constitutes a winning personal statement and almost all of them have some level of validity.

To begin with, how can you tell 86,150 annual applicants with 86,150 different personalities and backgrounds that there is one correct way to write a personal statement? You can't. Even if a small percentage of those applicants read and come to believe that a certain way is the correct way, it automatically becomes incorrect, because law schools despise getting personal statements that sound all too familiar—that are, in other words, impersonal.

In this chapter, we'll look at the procedure of putting together a personal statement. We'll share a list of DOs and DON'Ts that admissions officers most frequently mention. Then we'll show you some sample personal statements and provide critiques of those essays by real law school admissions officers. But keep one thing in mind: Because this is a personal statement, it cannot be modeled on something you see in a book. This section provides guidelines to follow, but the essay itself has to come from you.

PRESSED FOR TIME? HAVE QUESTIONS?

Kaplan Admissions Consulting provides personal, one-to-one admissions advice. We help you:

- Select appropriate schools and programs
- Develop polished applications
- Brainstorm and create winning essays
- Master the art of interviewing
- Deal with special circumstances

For more information about Admissions Consulting, call 1-800-KAP-TEST or visit kaptest.com.

KAPLAN)

Next to your LSAT score and GPA, the personal statement is probably the most important part of your application. If your numbers are excellent or very poor, it may get only a cursory glance. But if your numbers place you on the borderline at a school, then the essay may very well make the difference between acceptance and rejection. Personal statements are especially important at the top schools, because the number of qualified candidates makes it harder to choose. So many of the applicants to top schools have impressive GPAs and LSAT scores that admissions officers have to look at other factors, particularly the personal statement.

ESSAY TYPES

The personal statement is exactly what its name implies—a statement by you that is meant to show something about your personality and character. But don't be confused by this. It's not meant to be a lengthy essay detailing every aspect of your life since birth, and it's not intended to be a psychological profile describing all of your character attributes and flaws. Law school admissions officers can learn a lot about a person's character and personality from a simple story or even from the tone of the essay. In some instances the best essays are only remotely related to the applicant. The personal statement may just be an essay concerning a book the applicant recently read, or something she observed on television.

The point is that you need not write an in-depth personality profile baring your innermost soul. Admissions officers are adept at learning what they want to know about you from your essay, even if it doesn't contain the words "me," "myself," and "I" in every sentence. One exception, however, should be noted. Although most schools still provide wide latitude in their directions about what the personal statement should be about, some schools are becoming more specific with their requirements. For example, some schools now ask that you write about a particular achievement that you feel has been of personal significance to you; others ask you to describe any unique qualities you have that relate to your aptitude to study law. The problem with requirements like these is that you may well have to write a separate essay for that school alone. Be sure to check the instructions for every school to which you apply carefully and follow them closely. If a law school asks for a specific type of essay and you provide them with a more general one, they'll likely feel that you're not very interested in attending their school. But take heart. Most schools provide few restrictions on what you can write about, so unless you're very unlucky, you should be able to limit the number of essays you must write to two or three.

GIVE IT TIME

Start drafting your personal statement early in the application process, so that you'll be able to put it aside for a few weeks or even months. You'll be amazed at how different it will look when you go back to it. Sentences that seemed catchy when first written may appear clunky when read again a month later. Revisiting your essay after a period of time will allow you to read it with fresh eyes so you can make any necessary improvements or corrections.

> **PRIMARY PURPOSE**
>
> The personal statement is where you can best establish a theme for your entire application. A theme also will help keep your statement focused.

ESSAY LENGTH

How long should the personal statement be? Some schools place a word limit on the essay; others specify one or two typed pages. Always follow the specific directions, but you should be in good shape with virtually all schools if your essay is one and a half to two pages in length. Any shorter than this makes it more difficult for the reader to evaluate your personality. Any longer and your reader may go from interested to bored by the end. Obviously, an essay that runs a little longer than two pages is fine. But beware the three-, four-, or five-page essay. Unless your experiences or style justify the extra length, you may find yourself dismissed as long-winded and boring. Better to keep your essay to around two pages.

If you find that your essay is running long, check to see if you are inadvertently using filler words or wordy phrases. Review Maxim 3 in Chapter 2 on page 57 for more help.

ESSAY WRITING

The personal statement cannot be written overnight. Quite the contrary: A strong personal statement may take shape over the course of months and require several different drafts. One practice that we've found particularly effective is to write a draft and then let it sit for four to six weeks. The passage of time can provide you with an interesting angle through which to view what you've written. If you leave your essay alone for a significant period of time, you may find (to your astonishment) that your first instincts were good ones; on the other hand, you may shudder at how you could ever have considered submitting such a piece of garbage. Either way, time lends a valuable perspective; take advantage of it and start writing your essay early.

Try to start your essay sometime during the summer before you must submit your applications. Allow at least three months to write it, and don't be afraid to take it through numerous drafts or overhaul it completely if you're not satisfied. Engage several different readers to review your essay. Ask close friends or relatives to scrutinize it to see if it really captures what you want to convey. Be sure to ask them about their initial reaction as well as their feelings after studying it more carefully. Once you've achieved a draft that you feel comfortable with, try to have it read by some people who barely know you or who don't know you at all. Such people may include pre-law advisors at your school, professors not familiar with your work, friends of friends, or even professionals who charge a fee for reading and advising on essays. Strangers or semi-strangers often provide interesting perspectives on your work.

Since they haven't heard the story before and don't know the characters, they're often better able to tell you when something is missing or confusing.

Bottom line: Let a reasonable number of people read your essay and make suggestions. If certain criticisms are made consistently, then they're probably legitimate. But don't be carried away by every suggestion every reader makes. Stick to your basic instincts because, after all, this is your personal statement, and no one else's.

LINE 'EM UP

Try to line up as many people as possible to read and comment on your personal statement. Don't be swayed by everything that every person says, however. Listen to all comments, but take them to heart only if you really think they're valid.

Proofreading

It cannot be stressed enough: Proofreading is critical. Again, don't be afraid to enlist the aid of others. If possible, let an English professor review the essay solely for word choice and grammar mistakes. Law schools receive numerous complaints from practicing attorneys about law students who don't possess even fundamental English skills and writing ability. As a result, the schools are keeping a close eye on writing basics. And every time you revise your essay, be certain you use the spell check feature on your computer.

But don't rely solely on the spell check feature to catch every spelling error. Certain words might be spelled correctly but incorrect because of their usage. So always rely on human eyes to proofread your essay and make sure it is error free.

Brainstorming Exercises

Deciding what to write about for a personal statement can be as difficult as actually writing it! If you find yourself with a case of writer's block, don't let it get you down. Here are some tips for overcoming writer's block and beginning the important process of writing your personal statement.

If you're having a difficult time deciding on a topic, think of stories first.

Most people have stories about themselves that they repeat to more than one person. Granted, many of these aren't appropriate personal statement material—but if you keep the guidelines in mind, you may find an appropriate anecdote that ties into what you want to say. Asking friends and family for suggestions may also help.

Try focused free writing

Free writing is a technique often used by writers to get at what might evade them in a more polished draft. In free writing, you set a time (say, 15 minutes) and a topic (maybe, why you decided to go through the madness-inducing law school admissions process). When the clock starts ticking, you begin writing whatever comes into your head. The following topics are good places to start for focused free writing. Do even more of it, if you can. Free writing turns off the "mental editor" and allows you to get at different ideas and directions in an indirect, and perhaps more creative, way.

1. What are your three most significant accomplishments, and why does each one make this list?

2. Jot down two funny stories—preferably self-deprecating ones—that happened to you during the last five years.

3. You are going on a cross-country automobile trip and your car stereo is broken. With the prospect of endless stretches of lonely highway ahead of you, name three traveling companions— real or fictional— you'd want to take along, and explain why you chose them.

4. List one significant event that has had a dramatic impact on your thinking and describe that impact.

5. What makes you unique? Write at least 100 words.

6. What are two things about which you feel strongly—that get you motivated or fired up?

7. Name one major failure you have had, or mistake you have made, and describe what you learned from it. (If you can give two examples, do so.)

8. You are 80 years old, looking back on your life. In what ways do you consider yourself to have been a success?

9. If you had college to do over again, what would you do differently, and why?

10. Where do you see yourself five years from now?

11. Where do you see yourself ten years from now?

12. Choose one law school in which you are interested and write down at least two detailed and specific reasons for your interest.

Keep in mind that brainstorming is best done over time. Put away your responses to the brainstorming exercises for a day or two. Then reread them and write whatever comes to mind as a result.

KAPLAN

MAKING THE CONTENT GREAT: ESSAYS DOS AND DON'TS

We now move to the content of the personal statement. As stated earlier, there's no one correct way to write an essay, but admissions officers do provide some helpful tips about what they like and don't like to see in a personal statement. Let's begin with a list of the things that admissions officers most often mentioned they disliked seeing.

Essay DON'Ts

Avoid the Résumé Approach

This is the personal statement that begins at birth and simply recites every major (and sometimes minor) event of the person's life. Most of this information is repetitive since it's included on other parts of the application. But worse than that, it probably doesn't answer the question being posed. Bland list making is a common mistake made by applicants in their personal statements, and typically results in a very cursory read by the admissions officer. Unless your numbers are outstanding for a particular school, don't use this approach.

I'VE ALWAYS DREAMED OF BECOMING A LAWYER . . .

The first impulse of most people when writing the personal statement is to talk about their reasons for wanting to go to law school. That's a good reason why you shouldn't. Admissions officers read a hundred such essays a day. So, unless the application specifically asks for that topic, you should consider writing about something else.

Avoid the "Why I Want to Go to Law School" Essay

Although this can be a part of a law school essay, too many people make it the entire focus of their statement. The problem is that there are not many new variations on this theme, and the admissions officers have likely heard them all before, probably many times. You really don't need to convince them of your earnest desire to go to law school. What person in their right mind would go through this hassle if they didn't really want to go?

Avoid the "I Want to Save the World" Essay

Most applicants feel that they can accomplish some good by getting a law degree; very few are strictly mercenary. Admissions officers understand this and don't need to be convinced of your good intentions. Furthermore, overly idealistic essays can be very damaging if your record shows no previous commitment to public service. This kind of discrepancy can make the essay seem insincere. This doesn't mean, however, that if you do have a genuine, specific public-service goal in mind—and you've shown interest in it before law school—that you shouldn't discuss it and why it is important to you. Just remember that you're playing to a fairly skeptical audience.

Avoid Talking about Your Negatives

The personal statement is not the place to call attention to your flaws. Don't forget that you're selling yourself in your law school application, and the personal statement is your most prominent sales tool.

Don't Be Too Personal

Stories of abuse or trauma are often very moving and can be particularly effective if tied into a person's reason for wanting to practice law. Several admissions officers, however, have noted a trend toward describing such problems in graphic detail in personal statements. This kind of confessional essay can easily cross the line and become too personal. If you do decide to go this route, just remember that graphic details are not important; what's important is to show how the trauma affected you and your future plans.

SAVE IT FOR OPRAH

Confessional essays can easily cross the line and become too personal. Use this personal statement approach with caution.

NOT ANOTHER ALBERT SCHWEITZER!

Admissions officers hear about a lot of noble intentions in personal statements. Naturally, they're skeptical of such claims, especially if the rest of your application demonstrates no such selfless impulse. So be careful with protestations of high ideals. If you can't back them up with hard evidence, they're bound to come off sounding empty and insincere.

Watch the Use of Fancy Vocabulary

Don't try to impress the law school with your command of the English language. First of all, the trend in law these days is toward simpler, more easily understood language, with less "legalese." Moreover, misusing a 20-dollar word can be very embarrassing and costly.

Don't Discuss Legal Concepts

Along those same lines, don't try to engage the reader in a deep legal discussion to show how much you already know about the law. The school assumes that they can teach you what you need to know, regardless of the level at which you start. By discussing a legal concept, you also run the risk of showing a certain amount of ignorance about the subject, while at the same time appearing arrogant enough to have tried to discuss it.

Avoid Immature Subjects

Most applicants are at least in their early twenties and should be mature adults. Therefore, a story discussing a drunken evening from last summer, or your escapade to the local strip joint, is not appropriate. Law school officials are certainly aware of youthful excesses, but they're not particularly impressed if you consider yours important enough to discuss in your essay.

Don't Put Down Lawyers or the Legal Profession

Although it may seem that spewing cynicism about the legal profession is a clever device, trust us when we tell you that it isn't! The legal profession's attitude toward its members is similar to that of the fraternity member in the movie *Animal House* who, after seeing one of their pledges disgraced, said, "Nobody can do that to our pledges. Only we can do that to our pledges." Once you become a member of the legal profession, you can make as many lawyer jokes as you want. Until then, watch your step.

Shy Away from the Bizarre

It's true that law schools claim to value creativity, but some applicants confuse being creative with being outlandish. Shock value doesn't work. Although you do want to stand out from the crowd, imitating David Lynch is not the way to do it.

ESCHEW LEXICAL PROFLIGACY

Don't try to impress your reader with lots of difficult words. You'll come across as pretentious and, worse, you run the risk of misusing words, which will make you come across as ignorant.

NO LAUGHING MATTER!

You may think it'll come across as refreshing when you put down lawyers and the law profession in your personal statement. It won't. Your reader won't be amused.

Don't Try to Cover Too Many Subjects

Focus on one or two areas that you really want to talk about. One of the worst mistakes applicants make is to write essays that ramble from one subject to another and back again. Fight the desire to talk about every highlight of your life.

Now that you've got a sense of what not to do in your personal statement, let's turn to a list of suggestions for things that you should do.

Essay DOs

Tell Stories

Readers respond much better to a concrete story or illustrative anecdote than to an abstract list of your attributes. Instead of writing how determined you are, for instance, tell a story that demonstrates it. Courtroom attorneys always emphasize the importance of creating a story for the jury rather than just relating the facts. Why? Because stories stick in people's memories. The same holds true when you're trying to make sure the admissions officers remember you.

WINNING ESSAY EXCERPT

Competitive gymnastics training grew harder and harder as I became older. When I was sixteen years old I tore the rotator cuff in my left shoulder. Due to my age, my doctors did not want to operate. Instead, I went to physical therapy four times a week for five months. One year later, I fractured a vertebra and stopped training for several months due to intense pain. After each setback, I returned to the gym with a burning desire to compete and to qualify for the Junior National Championships. I never gave up . . . .

Make It Interesting

Before you decide what to write about, try to picture yourself as an admissions officer who reads hundreds—perhaps thousands—of essays in a six-month period. In the middle of the afternoon, having already read ten essays on how the applicant has wanted to be a lawyer since the age of four, imagine how great it is to come across an essay that grabs your interest for a few minutes. In moments of candor, admissions officers admit that these essays are few and far between, but are very welcome when they do appear. As mentioned earlier, many of the most interesting essays are only peripherally about the applicant; instead they may talk about a book or some current event or even some funny story the applicant heard. This is one reason it's so important to let others read your essay. Get an honest opinion from them on whether or not the essay truly interested them and held their attention.

WINNING ESSAY EXCERPT

While sitting outside my apartment complex waiting for my father to arrive, I was asked if I had a green card. The police officer questioned me, a 14-year-old Puerto Rican, about my immigration status and my involvement, if any, in a prior night's criminal activity. Incidents such as these have increased my desire to learn the law and use my knowledge to benefit my community . . . .

Be Funny—If You Can Pull It Off

Humor, particularly self-deprecating humor, is an effective device. Law applicants tend to be life-and-death serious, so admissions officers appreciate occasional flashes of irony. However, be careful in your use of humor. Check with others to make sure that any attempted humor works. Don't overdo it: A couple of funny lines or a funny story can be great, but include too many jokes and you start to sound flippant. Finally, think about using self-deprecating humor. Law schools often complain about the lack of humility among students and appreciate those who show some.

WINNING ESSAY EXCERPT

I went to my local bookstore the other day and noticed that Black's Law Dictionary *was shelved next to* Teach Yourself Sanskrit! *The possibility that this placement was deliberate has not deterred me from wanting to study law . . . .*

Start with a Great Lead

In private moments, admissions officers will often admit that they don't read every essay carefully. They may just glance at an essay to get a general impression. That's why it's important to grab them from the beginning. Let them see that this is not the run-of-the-mill personal statement. Start with a joke or story. Tell the ending of a story first and make them want to read on, to see how it all started. Begin with an interesting question that they'll want to see your answer to. Remember that your essay should not be more than one and a half to two pages and won't take them more than a few minutes to read. Make them want to take the time to read it carefully by grabbing them from the beginning.

Be "Unique"

The term *unique* has been overused. Even some applications now ask you to describe what is "unique" about you. Applicants rack their brains trying to figure out how they're different from the other 5,000 people applying to that law school. Or worse, some interpret unique to mean "disadvantaged," and rack their brains trying to think how they have suffered more than others. But what the admissions officers want to know is what qualities or experiences in your life would make you a particularly valuable member of a law school class. A major part of the learning process in law school is interacting with your classmates. Let them know what you would bring to that class, that is, your interesting perspectives and strengths, not necessarily what makes you different.

WINNING ESSAY EXCERPT

While I sought the advice of professional counsel for this acquisition, I also enjoyed doing my own due diligence in an effort to minimize costs and further educate myself on how businesses are bought and sold. I researched tax implications as a result of the possible transfer of ownership to an outside third party and the necessity of competition restrictions. In the course of my business experience, I have greatly improved my mediation ability and learned to listen to others before addressing their concerns.

Have a General Theme

The main point here is not to ramble. A general theme helps avoid that kind of drift and also creates at least the appearance of a well-organized essay. A theme can also give you a good way to begin and end the essay. Don't feel that you have to stick rigidly to your theme in every paragraph, but instead use it as a kind of organizing idea for your essay. Outlining can help you remain focused on your theme. We covered the importance of an outline for your LSAT Writing Sample in Chapter 3. You can use the same techniques described there for your personal statement.

KAPLAN)

Don't Be Afraid to Express Opinions

Applicants tend to shy away from stating political views or opinions. They worry that the reader will hold the opposite view and reject them automatically. But the opposite is usually true. Law schools are looking for people with a lot of different ideas, from all parts of the political spectrum, in order to create an exciting intellectual atmosphere. Don't be afraid to express your views. But, again, don't overdo it; you don't want to come across as offensive.

SHE'S SO UNUSUAL

Admissions officers aim to build a law school class that includes a rich variety of experiences and points of view. Think of the admissions officer as trying to assemble a symphony orchestra, with excellent players in every section: strings, woodwinds, brass, and percussion. Let them know what you could contribute to the diverse intellectual atmosphere they're trying to achieve.

Tailor Your Statement to a Particular Law School

If you're especially interested in a law school because they offer a particular program or professor, be sure to talk about that in your personal statement. Let the admissions officers know that their school is number one on your list, and make sure you explain why. Schools will appreciate that you took the time to research their strengths or specialties. This kind of specific enthusiasm also lets them know that you'll probably accept any offer of admission they may care to extend you.

WINNING ESSAY EXCERPT

Given my interest in international law, I am particularly excited about the prospect of attending Tulane and participating in one of your many summer abroad programs.

Open Up a Little

No, you don't have to bare your soul to these strangers, but don't be afraid to let them know a little about yourself. A bit of emotion or excitement or even embarrassment is not bad for them to see. Granted, two pages isn't a lot of space to show your deepest feelings, but neither should you completely hold back for fear of appearing wimpy.

> ## WINNING ESSAY EXCERPT
>
> *Last year, I spent a semester studying abroad in Paris, France. While I had traveled away from home before, that was the first time that I felt the full burden of responsibility for my life and for my actions. Handling my problems no longer involved just a short drive up Interstate 95 from Washington, D.C, to my parents' home in New Jersey. When I arrived in Paris, I became acutely aware of how out of place I was and realized that I had no one to turn to except myself . . . .*

SAMPLE PERSONAL STATEMENTS REVIEWED BY EXPERTS

The following sample personal statements were actually submitted by real law school applicants. Each sample statement is followed by feedback from admissions officials from the University of Texas Law School and Georgetown Law Center. Looking at sample statements and the accompanying critiques will give you a sense of what worked and what didn't work for other students. This might help you make some decisions about your own work. Keep in mind that the personal statement that will work best for you is the one that is uniquely your own, however.

> ## BE PERSONAL
>
> These samples will give you an idea of what an effective personal statement is like. Remember that a personal statement is *personal;* yours must come from you.

Sample Statement A

George behind the counter thinks I'm nuts. In a booth in the back of the diner, I sit from 5:30 A.M. until the library opens at 9:00 A.M., typing away on my laptop and drinking coffee, black. This is not the first time I've sat in this particular booth, and every time I do, George pours the refills and asks me the same question: "What are you doing awake at this hour?" The reason is simple. When the opportunity to participate in the betterment of the public interest presents itself to me, I invariably give my all without reservation. Perhaps this is what you get when you combine the altruism of my mother (an art teacher and unapologetic liberal) with the drive of my father (a Naval Academy graduate and straight commission salesman). I find that when working or teaching in the pursuit of the public interest, the

only thing which exceeds my devotion is my endurance. After graduating college with a degree in psychology, I found myself employed at a local mental health center. My duties included managing a caseload of 10–15 patients, each diagnosed with a major mental illness. One particular case involved a 43 year old who, affected by schizophrenia, had ordered 25 subscriptions from various magazines and $500 worth of food from The Swiss Colony. She was unable to pay these (and other) debts, and her meager income from disability would never provide her with the means to do so. For weeks, I spent every morning at the diner, writing letters to her various debtors. I tried to explain that their repeated and unrealistic demands for payment were only exacerbating her already extreme paranoia. After several months, I was referred by a colleague to the Mental Health Law Project, a nonprofit group of lawyers who devote themselves to protecting the interests of the mentally ill in New Jersey. An attorney from the group was able to accomplish more in 15 minutes than I had with my weeks of worry and dozens of letters. This experience planted a seed in my mind. A seed which sprouted the application you are now examining. I now believe there are two places in this society where one can effectively enact lasting social change: the classroom and the courtroom. One year ago, I set my sights on beginning a relationship with both. Toward that end, I set three goals for myself. The first was to use my speaking and writing skills as an advocate for the public interest. Within the past year, I have served on the faculty of New York University and Ramapo College, have been published in Et Cetera: The Journal of General Semantics, and have debated one of my research interests on the national PBS program "World.Com." My second goal was to pursue further insight through my own graduate education at New York University. In addition to maintaining a GPA of 3.97, I was selected as research assistant by internationally renowned author Dr. *** for his newest book. My third and final goal is to bring the success I have found in an academic research setting to the courtroom, where theory combines with action to serve the public interest and render lasting social change. Thus, you are holding in your hand my application to *** University School of Law. You are clearly a school dedicated to producing the finest in public interest lawyers, a dedication embodied in your *** Center. From my volunteer work with the terminally ill, to my work at the mental health center, I have been at my best when pursuing the public interest. I am confident that my dedication to public service, combined with the outstanding experience of a *** legal education, will arm me with the resources to make a positive social impact through the American judicial system. In the past, I've tried to explain to George why I've been awake at 5:30 A.M. in the back of his diner. Perhaps even he will understand the importance of the answer which I now ask you to provide. "I'm studying law at ***."

Critiques of Sample Statement A

Admissions Official #1   Many applicants have adopted the method of opening with an anecdote and returning to it to wrap up the statement. This applicant uses the diner anecdote effectively, but not exceptionally. Essay A, without the context of the entire application, would reveal someone committed to public service—a dedicated individual. However, the reviewer will likely seek out additional evidence that applicant A's commitment to service is truly unique from that of other applicants. In some applications, that evidence will be found in a résumé or list of public service/community activities; in others, it may be found in letters of recommendation or additional statements. Since the goal of this essay is to persuade the law school that the applicant is unique because of his commitment to public service, the reader will want to determine if the claim is truly valid. The fact that he is employed by a mental health center and that he works so many extra hours to help his patients is strong evidence that his commitment is real.

This essay unnecessarily spends the first paragraph of the second page covering information that the reader will see in other parts of the application—the résumé and transcripts. Such a waste of limited space should be avoided. This applicant's essay provides strong evidence of public service and, when looked at in combination with the other pieces of the application, might present a compelling argument that public interest law will remain his focus. Most applicants should not express plans to practice in a particular area of the law, because those plans so often change. Law schools are more interested in learning about the experiences have made you the person that you are today. Applicants should also avoid the temptation to express the desire to become a lawyer so that they can "change the world." Applicant A is reasonable in his goals: using the system to make "positive social impact." I'd like to make an important point here. The personal statement for law school is not the time for applicants to take literary license. Sentence structure, punctuation, and spelling must be flawless. Eyes that have not read a particular statement before will catch every error. Those errors can be distracting to the reader and costly to one's quest for admission.

AN IMPORTANT NOTE

It is important to mention at the outset that different law schools may prefer different kinds of personal statements. Thus, my opinions may not express the views of other schools to which you are applying. Please read each institution's information carefully to determine what would be most persuasive for each application. It is likely that you will need to create more than one version of your personal statement.

—Admissions Official #1

Admissions Official #2 Really nice beginning. We read thousands of personal statements and it's really nice to be drawn into a story that opens with a different character than the applicant, and hear a different voice from the applicant's. Within the first two paragraphs, I already have a sense of the applicant's theme, his goals, and his family background. Well done. The anecdote about the patient is effective, although the seed metaphor stretches a little. Don't try too hard when writing a personal statement: Err on the side of understatement.

The transition to the applicant's credentials is smooth. One small point: There is no need to get into specifics on your GPA. For one thing, I can find that information elsewhere. For another, it sounds unnecessarily defensive. This applicant does a good job in referring to the individual law school. If you are able to make your statement school-specific without seeming forced, go for it. Believe it or not, even we admissions officers love to be loved.

Nice finish. The applicant has managed to let me know him better by being himself and using language that is informal, conversational, and most importantly genuine. In addition, the applicant has made his involvement in public interest seem real by talking about a specific experience and not being heavy handed about saving the world. Really good job—this applicant has definitely helped himself.

FIVE WAYS TO HELP YOUR CAUSE

Admissions Official #2 gives these tips for writing an effective personal statement.

1. Try very hard to be the writer and reader at the same time. Imagine that you're sitting in an admissions officer's chair, charged with reading thousands of these, and then evaluate your work.

2. Stay focused and to the point. Have you ever heard, "Sorry to be writing you such a long letter, but I didn't have time to write you a short one"?

3. Give your statement to a friend and ask if she knows you better than before she read it.

4. Be yourself and trust your own voice.

5. Don't explain your weaknesses in the personal statement; it inevitably sounds too defensive. Use an addendum instead.

Sample Statement B

By the time I completed my doctoral exams in the History Department at *** University, my research interests as a graduate student had led me to desire a rigorous legal education. When I began my graduate studies, I planned to focus upon the historiographical issues surrounding the rise of Islam and the earliest Islamic centuries. Due to the legal nature of the surviving sources for this early period, my interests subtly changed over time to reflect the body of material I studied. As I began to translate and analyze Islamic legal sources, I found that I had to confront theoretical issues of jurisprudence in addition to considering the historical milieu in which these documents were produced. For example, in studying fourteenth-century legal opinions (fatwas) from Morocco, I became increasingly interested in how Muslim jurists (muftis) created religious law through different authoritative sources, ranging from statements of the Prophet Muhammad and verses of the Koran, to the legal opinions of subsequent jurists. By weaving together these related sources, the muftis constructed a form of jurisprudence which not only arrived at a legal resolution to the case, but also demonstrated how religion and law could become harmonized and unified through legal discourse. In order to augment my understanding of Islamic law and legal theory, I found it helpful to undertake a comparative approach and relate my findings to medieval European legal history and jurisprudence. For historians

of Islam, the evolution of canon law offers an alternative framework in which jurists have struggled to reconcile religious law with preexisting traditions. Moreover, these comparative studies have also challenged me to consider broader theoretical issues that are relevant to all legal systems, such as the relationship between formal legal codes and actual lived experience. In a course entitled "Conflict Resolution in Medieval Europe," I read Robert Ellickson's Order Without Law, *an analysis of how cattle ranchers in Shasta County, California, constructed their own norms of behavior independent of the former legal system. The culture of Shasta County is, of course, substantively different from medieval Islamic society; nevertheless, Ellickson's work invites Islamic historians to address the relationship between formal law and individual decision-making when assessing the significance of fatwas in the formation of Islamic civilization. Since completing my doctoral exams in 1996, I have returned to the specific topic of my dissertation research which concerns the origins of the Islamic trust, or* waaf. *Although I have a containing interest in this subject, I now believe that attending law school will offer me a greater opportunity to attain my personal and career goals. If I continue a career in academia as a legal historian, attaining a law degree will significantly enhance my ability to offer a comparative approach to Islamic law. A legal education will also improve my theoretical understanding of the relationship between law and society, and the subtleties of property law. And yet, despite my academic interests in the law, I recognize that a career as an academic historian may not be wellsuited to my broader life plans. Although I have attended summer programs in Jordan and Egypt, my wife and I remain uncertain whether we are prepared to endure longer periods of separation, or years of living abroad, in order for me to conduct the research necessary to continue my career as a medieval Islamic historian. In light of these concerns about pursuing an academic career, I am interested in exploring aspects of the legal profession, such as international law, which will allow me to combine my academic interests in the law with my knowledge of Islamic history and society. In applying to *** Law School, I have sought a program of study that would afford me the opportunity to pursue both my academic and professional interests in the law. The scholarly nature of the law program at *** complements my own academically oriented focus towards the law, while the school's commitment to training law students in the practice of law ensures that I will leave law school prepared for whatever path I may ultimately pursue. I believe that my knowledge of Islamic and medieval European law, as well as the analytical skills I have acquired in graduate school, will allow me to contribute a unique perspective to the law school classroom.*

Critiques of Sample Statement B

Admissions Official #1   This statement is very well written and is probably part of a strong application from an academic. However, it does not take full advantage of the opportunity presented. Applicants have a limited amount of space with which to sell themselves to admissions professionals and/or faculty. Each piece of the application should present new information to continue to add to the picture that the reader is developing, and it should be personal. We are looking for insight to who each applicant is as an individual. The discussion of Ellickson's book from the course, "Conflict Resolution in Medieval Europe," tells the reader nothing about Applicant B. I would prefer to see information about the applicant's performance in that class, and particularly about his written work for the class, in a letter of recommendation from the professor.

This essay nicely explains how the applicant's interest in law developed and how his current academic interests and research have led to legal studies. Although this applicant's motive for legal study is defined, that is certainly not always the case, and it is not a necessary part of a personal statement.

Applicant B also chose to discuss his career plans following law school. I admire the fact that he is willing to admit he is unsure where a law degree will take him. However, the issue did not need to be mentioned at all. In general, law schools are not interested in or persuaded by what an applicant claims she will do with a law degree because we recognize how often those plans change. There are occasions when an applicant's academic background or work experience show a true aptitude for and interest in an area of the law, and statements to that end can be effective, but only to the extent that the ambition seems to be consistent with the past experiences and academic background reflected throughout the entire application.

Finally, this essay is not a personal statement, but more of a topic paper which is not what law schools generally request. Some law schools may ask for an essay of this type to showcase writing ability, but the applicant should pay attention to the directions from each school. It is very important for applicants to provide each law school with the kind of information it requests. It may be appropriate to use one personal statement for School A, but not for School B.

THE 6 MOST COMMON MISTAKES

Admissions Official #1 lists these as the most common mistakes appearing in personal statements.

1. Spelling and grammatical errors

2. Sending an essay to School B that says, "I really want to go to School A."

3. Putting résumé information in essay form

4. Focusing on the weaknesses of the application instead of submitting such explanations as separate addenda

5. Being too cute (e.g., submitting the statement in the form of a brief to the court)

6. Writing a statement that is not personal and does not reveal information about the applicant

---

Admissions Official #2   Applicant B's opening is lifeless and worse, it promises to be about his specific area of study rather than who he is. While this applicant may find Islamic law and history interesting, the truth is that most of us do not read these things to be educated about anything except who the applicant is. The applicant's choice of topic and use of language make it really hard to get through this statement, especially considering how many statements we read. In writing on this topic, the applicant should have touched on the lighter aspects of its importance to him.

Now that I am finished reading, I really can't say that I know the applicant better than I did before I read it. Remember: I have your application at my fingertips. I suspect that I could learn most of what the applicant has covered here from his transcript and letters of recommendation. The language is much too dense, as is the topic. I'd advise this applicant to put himself in an admissions officer's place. After reading this, would he say, "This is exactly who we need at this law school"? Neither would I. In short, back to the drawing board.

Sample Statement C

My eyes burned as the wind gust sent a wave smashing into my face, forcing another mouthful of salt water down my throat. After three years of attending to crying kids with jellyfish stings and of kicking nonresidents out of the private parking lot, I finally found out what being a lifeguard really entails. Of course, these two elderly men had to pick a cold, windy day with an unusually strong current and high tide to try to swim to the rocks a half-mile off shore. They were drowning. I felt helpless as the undertow pushed me further away from them and I saw their heads slip beneath the water once again. While my arms felt like lead and my legs seemed as if they would fall off, I gasped for a deep breath and continued on, knowing two lives were depending on me and a fellow lifeguard. I was determined to reach the men before they drowned. It is that same determination that has carried me through many challenges in my life. I squeaked into *** on a prayer and a shoestring. My SAT score was not dazzling. The school required me to start college in the summer term, a week before I graduated from high school, to prove that I could cut it academically. Nearly four years later, I will graduate in the top ten percent of my class. I entered college determined to succeed, but without a clear focus. I spent many days meeting with advisers exploring a broad spectrum of possible areas of study, and many nights poring over the course catalogue. By the end of my sophomore year, still unable to find a conventional major that suited me, an adviser and I hammered out a unique Letters, Arts, and Sciences major with a "legal studies" theme. This allowed me the freedom and opportunity to gain a broad background in several related subjects, including History, Political Science, Speech Communication, and Labor and Industrial Relations. I have minors in Spanish and Information Systems and Statistical Analysis. This field of study has enhanced my critical thinking, reading, writing, and speaking skills, all of which will be useful in law school. When an adviser told me last fall that I would be unable to get an internship at a law firm as an undergraduate, I grabbed the phone book and literally dialed every attorney's number listed. After several days of perseverance and rejection, I finally located the one lawyer in town who was willing to take me. The attorney and I then created our own program, and I convinced *** to give me academic credit. On the first day of the internship, after about a half hour in the law library, I discovered why most attorneys hire law students to be legal interns. I was overwhelmed. I spent the greater part of the day just trying to decipher the legal jargon with which I was completely unfamiliar. However, after the work I had gone through to get this internship, I was not about to give up. I soon gained the respect of the partners in the firm, which became evident by the increasingly challenging tasks I was given. My Spanish minor proved to be useful in translating letters written to the attorney for whom I worked by a client in jail who did not speak English. By the end of the semester I proved to be a capable and competent legal intern, as reflected by a grade of "A," and was told by one of the lawyers that I had accomplished much more than he thought possible by an undergraduate. More importantly, I left the law firm with a reaffirmed feeling that pursuing a career in law is the right thing for me. When I think about the obstacles I will face in law school, I know it will not be an easy road. Yet I also know that through hard work and determination to succeed, I will be able to overcome any challenges with which I am presented. I will not be satisfied with anything less. I drove myself to push on that day last summer on Long Island Sound, as the two men *kept disappearing below the water. I would not let my first and only rescue attempt end in a fatality. Somewhere deep in myself I found a second wind, and used every bit of energy left in my body to kick harder and faster. I grasped the men by the wrists and pulled them onto a rescue board with a fellow lifeguard. As I realized they were going to make it, I was finally able to breathe a sigh of relief.*

OVERCOMING ADVERSITY

The theme of overcoming adversity is a common one in law school personal statements. In Personal Statement C, the author describes his struggle and how it led him to want a legal career.

Critiques of Sample Statement C

Admissions Official #1 This essay focuses on showing the applicant to be a determined and per-severing person—a fighter. The lifeguard anecdote is very catchy and creates suspense by not disclos-ing whether the swimmers survive until the end. The anecdote also does a good job of introducing the theme of this statement—determination—and is followed by several other examples.

Although this style may be appropriate for some law schools, it may not be the ideal style for others. There is no single correct style for a personal statement. Law schools are not looking for any particular technique or formula, but rather want simply to learn as much as possible about the applicant. Whatever story or style allows that insight is the right one for that individual. In general, it is a good idea for an applicant to get a second opinion as to whether the anecdote and the statement as a whole work and accurately portray her.

Applicant C uses his performance on standardized tests as an example of how his determination has allowed him to overcome challenges. However, in most cases, the argument that the SAT was not predictive of one's abilities in undergraduate school and that the LSAT will be equally invalid in predicting law school performance is best made in a separate addendum, not in the personal statement. Personal statements should be positive and sell the applicant. Explanations of weaknesses detract from that positive attitude. Different schools view these arguments in different ways, and some addenda are more compelling than others.

Creating one's own major shows initiative and is a somewhat unique accomplishment. However, law schools do not need the personal statement to list the types of classes taken since we examine copies of all transcripts, and certainly reviewers are aware of what skills particular classes teach.

The internship was used well in essay C. The applicant subtly demonstrates his ability to use his knowledge of a foreign language and completes the picture by explaining what he gained from the overall experience. Many times specific events in one's life or particular stories from one's past are appropriate and revealing topics for a personal statement. Law schools are interested in how those events or experiences affected the applicant or what was learned from the experience. This applicant selected a manageable topic and attempted to focus on only a few examples from his background that he thought relevant. This is important. An applicant has only a limited amount of time and space in which to persuade a committee to admit him, and he must be sure to keep the reader's attention and pick a story or stories that can adequately be revealed in limited space.

Admissions Official #2 The opening might have worked had the applicant not used such overheated language. It's okay to open with a story but trust your facts without feeling the need to embellish them. The transition to the second paragraph is very awkward. The difficulty probably comes from equating the courage to save someone from drowning with the courage to improve one's LSAT score. It feels much too melodramatic. The middle parts of the statement are essentially reduced to listing things that I could find elsewhere in your resume, transcript, and letters of recommendation.

Statement C contains a promising theme of the applicant's ability to persevere and work hard. However, the applicant needs to find a way to develop it without repeating what the admissions officer already knows and without making it seem like life and death.

Bottom line: Now that I am done, I know more about what the applicant has done rather than who he is. The applicant should use *I, me,* and *my* less when he reworks this. Overusing these words makes the applicant sound far too self-involved and self-important. I know that the applicant must write about himself in the personal statement, but a light touch is so much more effective.

THE 5 MOST COMMON MISTAKES

Here are the top five mistakes that have emerged from Admissions Official #2's experience of reading thousands of personal statements.

1. Too many adjectives and big words
2. Simply giving us information we have elsewhere—a paragraph form of your résumé
3. Staying too detached in writing style—this thing is called a "personal" statement, not just a statement
4. Claiming that you are the one who, if we just accept you, will in fact save the world
5. Piling a lot of information on us and assuming that we will sort out what we want. There are too many of you and not enough of us!

A FINAL TIP

The above points are as much general advice as we can responsibly give about the personal statement. We hope that they'll provide you with some ideas or keep you from making some costly mistakes. In the end, however, it is your personal statement, and it must come from you. But if you start early and enlist the aid of a variety of readers, your personal statement will be a breeze!

NOTES

NOTES

NOTES

NOTES

NOTES

NOTES

NOTES

NOTES

The Key to 1L Success

You made it to law school! The success you have had as an undergrad will translate into law school. Right? Not so fast. No matter what your background and success habits were as an undergrad, law school is different. It is as different as college was from high school. The faster you embrace the differences the better your chances are of success in law school. You may be smart, but so is everyone else.

Don't let this unnerve you. You've got Kaplan PMBR on your side to help you succeed. We provide invaluable guidance for all three years of law school, and *then* we help you pass the Bar Exam. Kaplan PMBR offers the most realistic, complete, up-to-date, and effective bar review prep through live courses, home study material, and small group tutorials. The following pages provide just a small preview of the insights and advice, tools and tactics that you'll receive in Kaplan PMBR's 1L Success Program. Visit our website at kaplanpmbr.com to learn more!

Your law school experience is likely to be the most challenging academic process of your life. Just remember, it can be done. Kaplan PMBR will help you do it. Good luck and we will see you on campus!

WHAT IS A "1L"? WHAT IS YOUR "SOL" ON YOUR "COA"? WHO IS THE "π"? WHO IS THE "Δ"?

If you answered these questions with a "Huh?" that is perfectly normal. Law school has its own language. A 1L is simply what first year law school students are called. "SOL" stands for statute of limitations. "COA" is your cause of action. π is shorthand for "Plaintiff", and Δ is shorthand for "Defendant". At first, it is a lot like learning Klingon, but you will learn quickly, and it is a language that will last you a lifetime. With a large legal dictionary in hand, you can create your own shorthand for note-taking and start using words like negate, moot, or sua sponte!

BE PROFESSIONAL

At first glance, law school seems to be very much like college. There are social events, a lot of studying, and new friends. However, keep in mind you are building a professional reputation that will follow you through the rest of your legal career. Your professors and classmates are learning who you are and those impressions last. Make sure they are good ones, and enjoy the process of becoming an attorney along the way.

NIGHT OWLS VS. EARLY BIRDS

Just because you've made it to law school doesn't mean you have to reinvent the wheel. In fact, don't. What and how you studied worked for you. If you study best at night, keep up that practice. If you study best first thing in the morning, continue to do so. Your study patterns have long been established and law school doesn't necessarily require you to change them. Stick with what works!

STUDY GROUPS AND STUDY MATERIALS

Two important issues you will face are whether you should join a study group, and when and how to use study aids.

Study Groups

Early in law school people usually scramble to get together to form study groups with other students. They are completely optional. Some groups will go fast, others slow. Others will study more of the social conditions in law school rather than anything substantive. To get the most from a study group, you must position yourself in the best group *for you*—should you choose to join one.

Study Materials

There are as many opinions about study aids. Used correctly, study aids can help you understand your class notes, let you see how things relate to each other, provide focus on the rationale of cases, and in the end, help you better understand the topic of law covered in class. Commercial outlines are prepackaged outlines in skeletal form of the law you need to know for a particular course. Hornbooks are the comprehensive and expansive overview of the particular course. They are also referred to as *treatises*.

Finally, there are the bar review programs. Don't let the term "bar review" fool you. True, Kaplan PMBR is a bar review company, but we also are a *law student* company. We have materials for first years, second years, third years, and *then* we help you pass the Bar Exam. For example, Kaplan PMBR offers substantive black letter law course outlines and audio CDs to help you prepare for classes. These are resources you will turn to again and again—throughout law school and beyond. Visit our website at kaplanpmbr.com to learn more or to enroll.

OUTLINES

What goes into an outline? Essentially, it contains the rules of law, exceptions, and defenses to it. As a brief example, a Battery is a harmful or offensive touching of another with Intent. Consent is a defense to battery.

You might choose to incorporate some of your professor's pet topics or the like to keep them in the front of your mind. They very well could show up on the exam. Sometimes students split up different sections of the course with each creating an outline for her or his portion. However, if you focus on only one portion of the course, you will likely have a good understanding of only that one area and must rely on someone else's perception of their section of the course. Make your own outlines for each course. This allows you to understand the material and how it relates together.

THE EXAM PROCESS

Your exam can include multiple choice questions, short answer, and most popular, essay questions. Your grade depends on how you perform on the exam. However, it is what you do prior to exam day that will have the most impact on your success. Developing a good outline, learning to spot issues, honing your exam skills by practicing on old exams, and designing your test strategy are all solid ways to get ahead of the game and likely many of your classmates as well.

Issue spotting

The first step is knowing the law. The next—issue spotting—is a real time test of your ability to identify legal issues or causes of action. Your professor will test you on material you covered in class and material you were assigned but didn't cover in class. Every law school exam is invented using complex situations that may involve multiple lawsuits or defendants, and usually the professor will ask multiple questions. Truly, some facts are trash while some are treasure. You'll have to decide which is which.

Practice Exams

Practice exams are an essential tool to building your law school success. Sample exams are an underappreciated and underutilized tool. Too often, in the heat of preparing for exams, they are overlooked or ignored due to time constraints. Not only are they are a great barometer of the issues the professor likes, the style of the exam, but you could luck out and one those questions could end up on your actual final exam. Remember to allocate the time to use them!

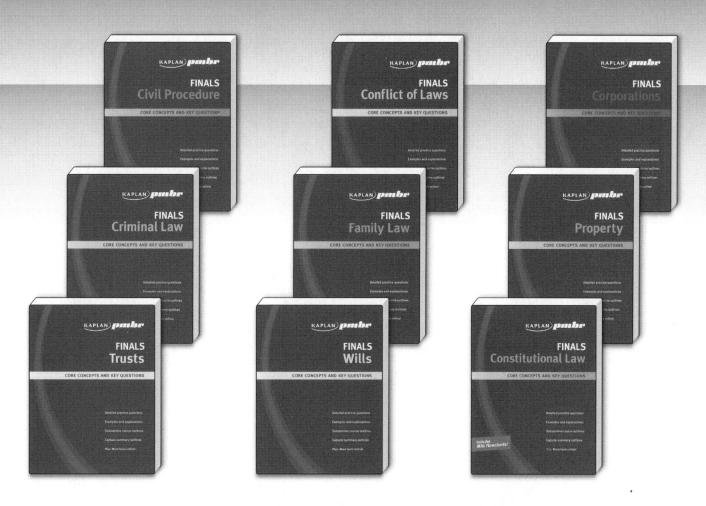